Creative Cooking with
SPICES

the
apple
press

Creative Cooking with
SPICES

WHERE THEY COME FROM & HOW TO USE THEM
J·A·N·E W·A·L·K·E·R

A QUINTET BOOK

Published by Apple Press Ltd.,
293 Gray's Inn Road,
London WC1X 8QF

ISBN 1 85076 052 7

This book was designed and produced by
Quintet Publishing Limited
6 Blundell Street, London N7

Art Director Peter Bridgewater
Editor Nicholas Law
Photographer Trevor Wood assisted by Michael Bull
Home Economist Brenda Smith assisted by Paula Smith
Illustrator Lorraine Harrison
The author and publishers would like to thank House
Food Industrial Company (Japan) for permission to
reproduce the illustrations on pages 6-12.

Typeset in Great Britain by
Q.V. Typesetting Limited, London
Colour origination in Hong Kong by
Universal Colour Scanning Limited, Hong Kong
Printed in Hong Kong by Leefung-Asco
Printers Limited

—Contents—

Introduction   6

The spices   13

Allspice   14

Aniseed   17

Caraway   20

Cardamom   23

Cassia   26

Cayenne   29

Chilli (chili)   32

Cinnamon   38

Clove   41

Coriander   45

Cumin   49

Curry   54

Fenugreek   57

Garam masala   60

Garlic   64

Ginger   69

Horseradish   74

Mace   77

Mustard   80

Nutmeg   84

Paprika   87

Pepper   90

Pimento   97

Poppy seed   100

Saffron   103

Sesame seed   107

Star anise   110

Turmeric   114

Vanilla   117

Sauces   120

Drinks   122

Spice mixes   124

Index   126

— INTRODUCTION —

SPICES ARE MORE than just a food, they are an idea which has both changed the course of history and enriched the very language which we speak. To 'spice it up,' 'the spice of life,' or just plain 'spicy' are words and phrases which suggest not merely specialness but the exotic; a little bit of fun; even the *risqué*.

Diversion, or the escape from boredom has remained a constant human quest which began long before history itself. People lacked books, telephones, televisions and so on, but they did have to eat. No wonder those tiny, but powerful packages of exotic pleasure came to be so cherished.

Growing everywhere — just outside the kitchen door, so to speak, were and are another group of plants used primarily to add flavour to other foods — the herbs. Of course, they have their own story, but it was always spices which triggered the passions of people and fired their imaginations.

So what are spices? Unfortunately, there is no absolutely clear, simple and universal definition. Surely some readers will find it rather strange that an introduction admits that the book's very subject matter is impossible to define. The problem is that nature does not operate for the purpose of neatness in botanical classification. Or, to put it another way, spices are a human concept rather than an immutable law of the universe.

There are, of course, a number of general statements which can be made about both spices and herbs. The first is that their use in food is primarily aromatic rather than nutritional. The spice or herb is used to flavour another food which forms the major part of the meal or dish. Exceptions exist even for this fundamental statement. There are a number of dishes for which garlic is cooked as a vegetable rather than treated only as a spice. Herbs, generally, are the green leafy bits and perhaps parts of the stems of aromatic plants, but what of spices? It is true that most often they are dried, while herbs are used in forms both fresh and dried, but the odd exception can be found even here. Spices come from virtually every conceivable part of plants: pepper and allspice (or pimento) are dried berries; cinnamon and its sister spice, cassia, are tree bark: ginger and turmeric are rhizomes: nutmeg is the kernel of the seed of an apricot-like fruit, while mace is the seed coating, or aril of the same fruit: chillis, vanilla and cardamom are all fruits themselves; and cloves are unripened flower buds. Incidentally, if the clove buds are not picked but left, they become lovely pink and fragrant blossoms, but are no longer cloves. And garlic... Some say garlic is not a spice, and others call it a herb. The plant does have spear-like green leaves, but that is not the part used as a flavouring.

In order to end the confusion, some writers, who must have been in dire need of something to think about, proclaimed that true spices had to grow in the tropics. They also invented a third category over and above herbs and

LEFT: *Garlic on sale in a market.*
BELOW: *Pickers removing the buds from the flower stalks of a tropical evergreen tree belonging to the myrtle family. The cloves are the dried unopened flower buds.*

spices called 'aromatic seeds.' This works perfectly well for, say, pepper, which everyone agrees is a spice and always grows near the equator. It does mean, though, that garlic, which grows in temperate regions, cannot be considered a spice, but it can hardly be called an aromatic seed when it is not even a seed! Before returning to the drawing board, perhaps we should agree that exact definitions really are not necessary and get on with the fun.

The earliest trading caravans transported salt, but even before the dawn of human history they were also carrying spices. The early civilizations of the Mediterranean and the Near East craved the spices of India and lands eastward. Records exist of Egyptian spice expeditions to the east coast of Africa between three and four thousand years ago. Particularly treasured were the two aromatic barks, cinnamon and cassia. The Egyptians used them not only to flavour foods but in cosmetics and an assortment of ceremonial functions including the important burial rites. Consider this excerpt from Exodus:

> Moreover the Lord spake unto Moses, saying, Take thou also unto thee principal spices, of pure myrrh five hundred shekels, and of sweet cinnamon half so much, even two hundred and fifty shekels, and of sweet calamus two hundred and fifty shekels. And of cassia five hundred shekels, after the shekel of the sanctuary, and of olive oil an him: And thou shalt make it an oil of holy ointment after the art of the apothecary: it shall be an holy annointing oil. And thou shalt anoint the tabernacle of the congregation therewith, and the Ark of the Testimony.

BELOW: *The cinnamon quills are prepared from the valuable inner bark, after the outer bark has been stripped off.*
RIGHT: *Ginger roots being sorted for purchase.*

Today calamus grows throughout Europe and America and is known as sweet flag or sedge. Myrrh of course, figures significantly in later biblical episodes, especially as a mild potion of love in the Song of Solomon and as one of the gifts brought by the wise men for the baby Jesus. The point is that they both still grow in the Middle East and have done so since ancient times. By contrast, cinnamon and cassia do not, nor ever have grown in the region, yet were commanded for the most sacred of duties, the ointment for the holy Ark itself. From where then did they come?

The ancient Greek historian Herodotus asked this very question and came up with the area around the Red Sea, which he called the 'cinnamon growing lands.' He wrote of great birds using the spice to build their nests and of Arabs coming near with large sides of meat. The birds would take the meat up to the nests which would break under the strain of its weight, allowing the Arabs to collect the cinnamon. According to the historian, cassia was collected by an equally bizarre plan in which snakes figured prominently.

It was left to the Roman historian Pliny the Younger to come close to the real story. Pliny's investigation of the matter arose because as a Roman treasury official he became

ABOVE: *Green berries are laid out in the sun to dry.*
RIGHT: *After the green berries have been dried for about 1½ weeks they turn into the familiar black pepper corns.*

alarmed at a crisis in the balance of payments. The luxury-loving Romans, in order to secure supplies of eastern spices, were sending vast amounts of gold out of the Empire in the direction of India. Pliny described a series of fantastic voyages across thousands of kilometres of open ocean, starting east of India and ending on the east coast of Africa. The cinnamon carriers, on tiny open rafts, used only the stars for navigation and often took as long as five years to complete a round trip. For their troubles, they took home bits of glass, bracelets and baubles. Remarked Pliny, referring to both the Romans and the remarkable spice sailors, '...hence it is, that this traffic depends chiefly upon capricious female fidelity to fashion.' It appears that the numerous Arab middlemen got most of the gold.

Had Pliny been a linguist he would have known that our word and the Roman word 'cinnamon' were derived from the almost identical Hebrew word used in the Bible which itself was derived from ancient Malay, meaning 'sweet wood.' To suggest some idea of the antiquity of this long-distance spice trade, consider the fact that the Roman, Pliny, lived and wrote closer in time to today than to the time of the Exodus! So Biblical cinnamon probably originated in the region of modern Malaysia. Cassia likely first came from the Khasi Hills of Assam, a region lying between the northern parts of Bangladesh and China. It could have been carried on packs

or by animals across the tortuous width of Asia itself by a trail which later would be called 'The Silk Route.'

So the spice trade is very ancient indeed. When Europeans were running barefoot through the woods dressed in animal skins, a thriving commerce between East and West flourished throughout the Indian ocean and Asia. Ultimately, that was destined to change.

The point about spices is that they travel and keep. They are their own best containers.

> The herbs were springing in the vale:
> Green ginger plants and liquorice pale,
> And cloves their sweetness offer,
> With nutmegs too, to put in ale,
> No matter whether fresh or stale,
> Or else to keep in coffer.

These words were written by an Englishman who lived between 1340 and 1400, Geoffrey Chaucer. His ginger could have come from India or East Africa, and the liquorice from southern Europe, but it is the cloves and nutmeg which have a story to tell. Remember in Chaucer's time European ships could scarcely venture into open ocean and only rarely out of sight of land. The idea of sailing around Africa would have been considered as madness. Nobody even knew if Africa had an end: indeed most people then had probably never even heard of Africa or the Indian Ocean.

Yet, at the time, all the cloves in the world came from a tiny group of islands lying on the equator between Borneo and New Guinea, the Moluccas, or Spice Islands. Even more astonishingly, all the world's nutmegs grew on an even tinier set of nearby islands known as Banda, known, that is, to the Indonesian and Arab traders who, for thousands of years, had come to the islands. Certainly, neither Chaucer, nor anyone else in England had the slightest idea of the area's existence.

Today it is almost impossible to imagine the epic journey across half the world's surface those spices had to make to end up in Chaucer's ale. No wonder he wrote: '...or else to keep in coffer.'

In Chaucer's time the magnificent and powerful city-state of Venice ruled the Mediterranean. Much of her wealth came from agreements made with Arab traders to control the spice trade. All the fabulous spices of the Orient flowing into Europe passed through Venice, as did vast quantities of gold and silver flowing eastward. The Venetians grew rich, but the rest of Europe began to suffer the same balance of payment crises which had so worried the Romans. Far to the west, in the tiny but newly independent kingdom of Portugal one man decided to challenge the supremacy of Venice. Ultimately, his decision changed the whole course of human events.

Prince Henry of Portugal's plan was simple: find the end of Africa, sail around it all the way to India, and buy the spices directly from the producers, cutting out the Venetians and the Arabs. In hindsight it seems mad. Henry might just as well have chosen the moon or Mars to sail to. But he was driven not only by his lust for spices, but his hatred of the Moslem Arabs and the hope of finding a fabled Christian empire in the East. He gathered the world's greatest scholars and navigators about him and set out upon his grand plan. Henry died before it was accomplished, but the Portuguese did develop new ships which could sail against the wind and new methods of navigation which let them venture out into the open ocean.

By the 1480s the Portuguese had rounded Africa and were ready for the final push upon India itself. This so worried Portugal's neighbour and rival, Spain, that the Spanish decided to finance an Italian navigator who claimed that he could reach India ahead of the Portuguese by sailing, not around Africa, but westward into the Atlantic. Christopher Columbus' astounding voyage was to alter everything, but more about that later.

ABOVE: *The nutmeg fruit showing the nut covered with mace.*

In 1497 the Portuguese reached their goal, India. Their leader, Vasco da Gama announced, so the story goes, 'I have come for Christians and spices.' It is worth noting that India would remain under European subjugation for the following 450 years! Columbus, of course, to his lasting disappointment never found India. He did find islands, continents and empires which his fellow Europeans were quick to claim as their own. For the next half a millennium, the dominant world geo-political fact would be European colonialism, and it all started with the search for the source of spices.

The discovery of the new world forever changed the eating habits of the old. It is difficult to imagine a pre-America Europe void of tomatoes, potatoes, chocolate, vanilla, maize (corn), peanuts and turkey. Columbus caused everlasting confusion by calling all the peoples he encountered Indians. Similarly, he continued to muddy the linguistic waters by bestowing upon two very different plants the name of yet a third, pepper.

The first 'pepper' he discovered boasted berries somewhat larger than the Indian variety, the 'Asian' Indian variety. Also, it possessed a glorious aroma at the same time reminiscent of cloves, cinnamon and nutmeg. This was dubbed 'la pimenta de Jamaica,' or Jamaican Pepper. Today it is called pimento by Jamaicans, but is known in its ground form as allspice.

Allspice or, if you prefer, pimento, is a marvellous spice used in a vast array of commercial foods. It is surprising that more people do not employ it in the kitchen.

It was, however, the other spice found by Colombus which set the culinary world on its ear. Capsicums in their many colours and varieties had been cultivated by the peoples of Mexico, Central and South America for no less than 9,000 years! Along came the lost sailor Colombus and called them 'pimientos' or 'peppers.' Today, we still call those large mild red and green capsiciums, along with the much smaller and hotter yellow and red varieties, peppers. In no way are they related to the sneeze-inducing powder which resides in the shaker beside the salt. To avoid confusion, we shall refer to the hot capsicums by a name derived from their native American cultivators — chillies (chilis). Incidentally, the name has nothing to do with the country Chile.

Aside from flavour, spices always have been called upon for pungency or heat. Until the European arrival of the chilli at the beginning of the 16th century, the spices used for pungency were pepper, mustard, horseradish and, perhaps, ginger. Each of these spices carries along with its heat an entire flavour complement. With chillies the additional flavour is minimal and piquancy can be obtained without upsetting other flavour balances. As they are easily cultivated, it is little wonder that the little hot fruits flourished wherever the Spanish and later Portuguese sailors went. Surely it was a great day in the history of food when the chilli arrived in India. Today, that country is the world's largest grower and it simply is inconceivable to consider Indian food without the heat of the chilli. So central is the chilli to Indian cookery that many there still refuse to believe that the plant is not native to the land but was brought by the Europeans. It is ironic that the quest for the spices of India finally led to the transformation of the food of India itself.

The two 'Christian' nations, Spain and Portugal, started to interfere with each other's conquests to such an extend that the Pope drew an imaginary line down the centre of the Atlantic ocean to separate their spheres of interest. Portugal could have all the heathen lands east of the line while Spain could take those to the west. It was not clear, however, from the early charts whether the Moluccas and Banda, the homes of cloves and nutmegs, fell into the Portuguese or the Spanish sphere of influence.

The Spanish felt that their claim would be strengthened if the islands could be reached by sailing westward and following Columbus's original plan. An expedition of five ships and two hundred and thirty men was mounted, led ironically, by a Portuguese, Ferdinand Magellan. They

journeyed westward into the Atlantic, down the coast of South America and finally into the Pacific ocean. The expedition did reach the Moluccas, but Magellan himself was already numbered amongst the many casualties. Three years after it set out, only one ship, with eighteen emaciated sailors aboard, finally returned to Spain. Undoubtedly, these eighteen were the very first human beings to sail around the world — for cloves and nutmegs!

The following century saw the decline of Spain and Portugal and the rise of new and ever more ruthless European empires: England, Holland and France. Great companies were formed to marshal the necessary capital to mount eastward expeditions. The Dutch, in particular, formulated and executed plans to corner the world market in various spices. They destroyed all the clove and nutmeg trees on Earth except for those growing on closely guarded islands. Ultimately cloves and nutmegs escaped to be cultivated elsewhere, breaking the Dutch stranglehold.

By the middle of the 18th century the desperate desire for spices was slowing down. In fact, the spices of choice were

OPPOSITE: *A field of croci being harvested.*

ABOVE: *Turmeric is sold in powdered form which quickly loses its aromatic qualities.*

RIGHT: *A selection of different types of rice, pulses and beans.*

changing. In the early years, cinnamon and cloves were most valued because the primary method of cooking in Europe was the single pot on the hearth, in which various foods of widely differing flavours were cooked together. There was no distinction between sweet, sour and savoury dishes. Both cinnamon and cloves are binding spices; they bring together the opposite flavour of sweet and sour. For example, apple strudel with sour apples and sweet sugar would be unthinkable without cinnamon or cloves or both.

The introduction of the cooking stove meant that everything no longer had to be cooked together. A new type of main dish arose, savoury, and with it a different spice took prominence — pepper. The new nation, the United States, entered the pepper trade with fast ships out of the New England port of Salem. Profits from the trade were used to build much of the state of Massachusetts' industrial base.

Finally, the arrival of eastern spices in abundance meant the decline of the local European spices, mustard and saffron. Mustard was destined for a number of renaissances, especially in the French town of Dijon and the English company of J.&J. Colman. But, alas, widespread saffron use never returned. Today saffron is cultivated principally in Spain where it is used in the local *paellas*.

Throughout the ages people have cherished spices not only for their flavour and piquancy, but their perceived benefit to health. It is only in relatively recent times that food and medicine have become separate and distinct. Each of the spices contain a number of often complex and powerful chemicals. Modern medical science makes no claims for the curative value of any of the spices, although we can take note that for thousands upon thousands of years people in every continent have extolled their virtues in this respect.

This book, however, will be primarily about food; about cooking with and using spices in the kitchen. Today spices

ABOVE LEFT: *It is vital to harvest the mustard seed crop when the seeds are mature but before the pods burst and the seeds are scattered.*

ABOVE RIGHT: *Green pimento berries which when dried are called allspice.*

are easier than ever to obtain. Any reasonable supermarket will have a wide variety, but mostly already ground. Spices in general should be kept in dry dark and airtight conditions, especially ground spices which should be used quickly. This then is a simple plea that whenever possible you should buy whole spices and grind them yourself.

As grinders and whole peppercorns become more and more popular, whole pepper becomes easier to use. Here's a hint: try mixing a few whole allspice berries in with your peppercorns, and use as you would ordinary pepper.

Do try fresh whole nutmeg. The 18th century saw nutmeg proclaimed as a wonder drug and people used to carry their own nutmegs and grinders around with them. We do not advocate anything so extreme, but there is no substitute for freshly ground nutmeg and it is as easy to grind as shaking a bottle. You should also become familiar with the lovely spice mace, in its aril form. In fact, experiment with all the spices and, above all, have fun. If things are becoming a little dull, why not spice them up?

THE
S PICES

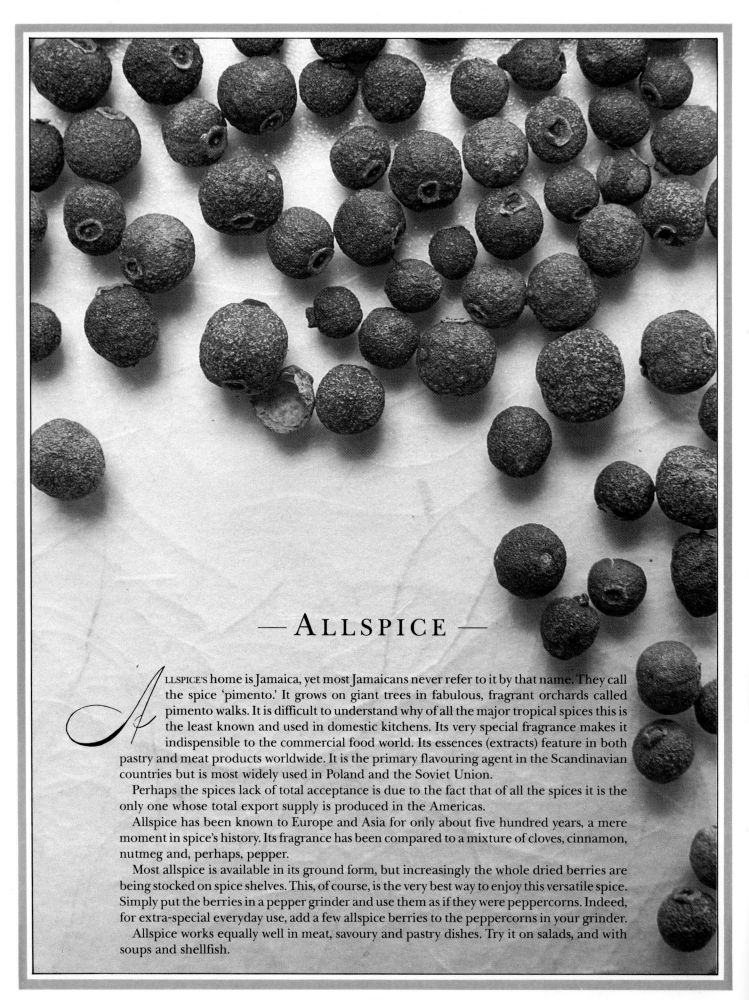

—ALLSPICE—

ALLSPICE's home is Jamaica, yet most Jamaicans never refer to it by that name. They call the spice 'pimento.' It grows on giant trees in fabulous, fragrant orchards called pimento walks. It is difficult to understand why of all the major tropical spices this is the least known and used in domestic kitchens. Its very special fragrance makes it indispensible to the commercial food world. Its essences (extracts) feature in both pastry and meat products worldwide. It is the primary flavouring agent in the Scandinavian countries but is most widely used in Poland and the Soviet Union.

Perhaps the spices lack of total acceptance is due to the fact that of all the spices it is the only one whose total export supply is produced in the Americas.

Allspice has been known to Europe and Asia for only about five hundred years, a mere moment in spice's history. Its fragrance has been compared to a mixture of cloves, cinnamon, nutmeg and, perhaps, pepper.

Most allspice is available in its ground form, but increasingly the whole dried berries are being stocked on spice shelves. This, of course, is the very best way to enjoy this versatile spice. Simply put the berries in a pepper grinder and use them as if they were peppercorns. Indeed, for extra-special everyday use, add a few allspice berries to the peppercorns in your grinder.

Allspice works equally well in meat, savoury and pastry dishes. Try it on salads, and with soups and shellfish.

— Allspice —

Curried Goat

SERVES 4

This is a famous Jamaican dish. Kid is normally used, but lamb is a very good substitute.

INGREDIENTS

1 kg/2 lb kid or lamb
5 g/1 tsp salt
5 g/1 tsp pepper
2 fresh hot red peppers, finely chopped
1 large onion chopped
5 g/1 tsp Curry Powder (see page 124)
30 ml/2 tbsp vegetable oil
2.5 g/½ tsp allspice berries
2½ cups/550 ml /1 pt water
1½ cups/200 g/½ lb diced potatoes

PREPARATION

◆ Clean and cut the meat into cubes. Season with salt, pepper, hot red peppers and chopped onion.
◆ Rub curry powder into meat and allow to stand for 1 hour.
◆ Heat the oil in a frying pan and fry meat briskly to brown. Add the allspice berries and water.
◆ Cover the pan and allow to cook very slowly until the meat is tender, about 2 hours.
◆ Add the diced potatoes and cook until the gravy thickens.
◆ Serve with rice or green bananas, or both.

Spiced Vinegar

INGREDIENTS

1 blade of mace
7 g/1½ tsp allspice
7 g/1½ tsp cloves
1 quill of cinnamon (piece of cinnamon stick)
6 black peppercorns
7 g/1½ tsp ginger fresh root, or hot pickled
6¾ cups/1½ l/2½ pt vinegar

PREPARATION

◆ Tie the spices in a muslin (cheesecloth) bag and place in a covered pan with vinegar. Heat slowly to boiling point.
◆ Leave to infuse for at least 2 hours and then remove bag.
◆ Leave pickle for at least 5 days before opening the jar.

Do not make too much at a time as the cabbage looses its crispness after 3 months.

Pickled Red Cabbage

INGREDIENTS

1 firm red cabbage, medium size
salt
6¾ cups/1½ l/3 pt spiced vinegar

PREPARATION

◆ Trim and quarter the cabbage, discarding discoloured leaves and central stalk. Cut into very fine strips.
◆ Place the shredded cabbage in a bowl with plenty of salt sprinkled over the layers. Leave overnight.
◆ Prepare the spiced vinegar (see below).
◆ Rinse the cabbage and drain thoroughly.
◆ Pack loosely into clean jars. Cover with spiced cold vinegar and tie down.

Honey Cake

INGREDIENTS

⅔ cup/150 g/6 oz sugar
2 eggs
30 ml/2 tbsp vegetable oil
⅔ cup/200 g/8 oz honey
2¾ cups/300 g/12 oz plain (all-purpose) flour
5 g/1 tsp baking powder
5 g/1 tsp ground ginger
5 g/1 tsp ground allspice
5 g/1 tsp bicarbonate of soda (baking soda)
½ cup/100 ml/4 oz warm water
blanched almonds for decoration
oven temperature 180°C/350°F/Gas 4.

PREPARATION

◆ Cream the sugar and eggs, add the oil and honey, and stir thoroughly.
◆ Sieve the flour, baking powder, ground ginger, allspice and bicarbonate of soda and add the honey mixture, alternating with warm water.
◆ Pour the mixture into a greased and floured bread tin (pan). The mixture should be of a loose consistency.
◆ Decorate with blanched almonds and bake in the oven for an hour.

This is a traditional cake for the Jewish New Year.

— Allspice —

Spice Cake

INGREDIENTS

1 cup/200 g/8 oz butter or soft margarine
½ cup/125 g/5 oz white sugar
½ cup/125 g/5 oz dark soft brown sugar
4 eggs, separated
2¾ cups/300 g/12 oz plain (all-purpose) flour
15 g/3 tsp baking powder
10 g/2 tsp ground allspice
10 g/2 tsp ground cinnamon
5 g/1 tsp ground nutmeg
1 cup/225 ml/8 fl oz water
oven temperature 190°C/375°F/Gas 5

PREPARATION

♦ Cream the butter or margarine with the sugars.
♦ Beat in the egg yolks, one at a time.
♦ Sieve together the dry ingredients and gradually add to the creamed mixture, alternating with the water.
♦ Beat the egg whites until stiff and gently fold them into the mixture.
♦ Turn the mixture into a well-greased 22.5-cm/9-in square pan.
♦ Bake in a preheated over for 40 minutes.
♦ Cool the cake for 10 minutes then turn out onto a wire rack.

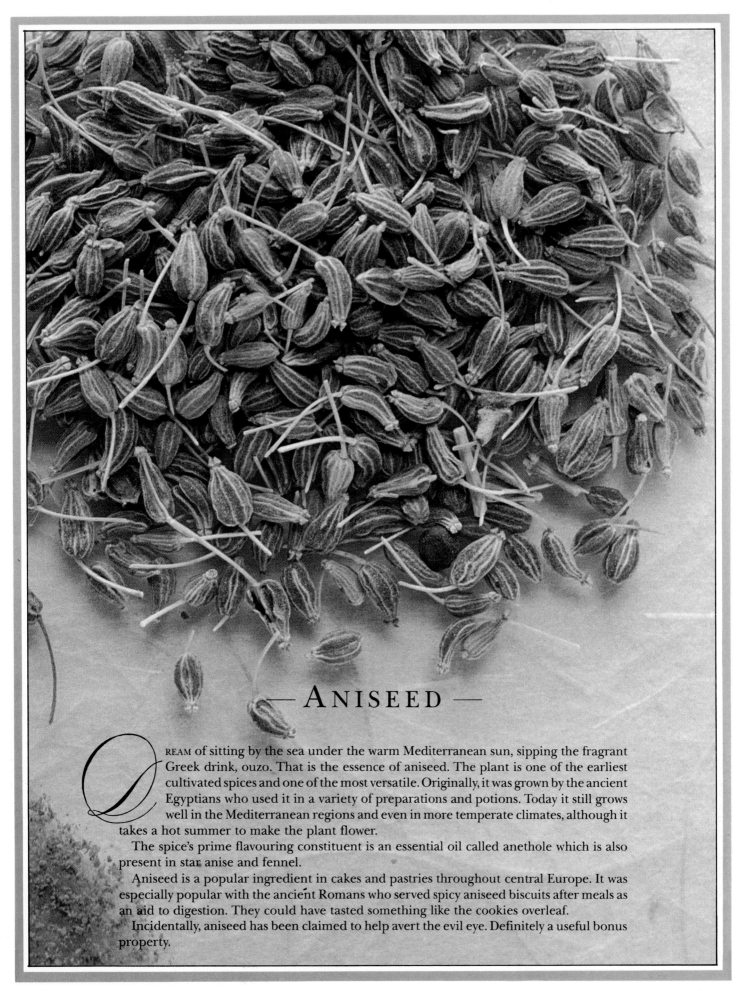

— ANISEED —

*D*REAM of sitting by the sea under the warm Mediterranean sun, sipping the fragrant Greek drink, ouzo. That is the essence of aniseed. The plant is one of the earliest cultivated spices and one of the most versatile. Originally, it was grown by the ancient Egyptians who used it in a variety of preparations and potions. Today it still grows well in the Mediterranean regions and even in more temperate climates, although it takes a hot summer to make the plant flower.

The spice's prime flavouring constituent is an essential oil called anethole which is also present in star anise and fennel.

Aniseed is a popular ingredient in cakes and pastries throughout central Europe. It was especially popular with the ancient Romans who served spicy aniseed biscuits after meals as an aid to digestion. They could have tasted something like the cookies overleaf.

Incidentally, aniseed has been claimed to help avert the evil eye. Definitely a useful bonus property.

— Aniseed —

Anise Cookies

INGREDIENTS
3 eggs
¾ cup/100 g/4 oz demerara sugar
6 dessertspoons/150 g/6 oz wholewheat flour
1 tsp/5 ml baking powder
1½ tbsp/20 ml/1½ oz finely ground aniseed
oven temperature 170°C/325°F/Gas 3

PREPARATION

♦ Beat the eggs until pale yellow.
♦ Add the sugar and beat for 3 minutes.
♦ Mix the dry ingredients together and fold into the mixture.
♦ Drop the mixture a teaspoonful at a time onto a well-greased baking sheet, allowing an inch between each.
♦ Leave to stand at room temperature for 18 hours.
♦ Bake in a preheated oven for approximately 12 minutes, or until cookies begin to colour.

— ANISEED —

Carrot and Sweet Potato Tzimmes

SERVES 6

INGREDIENTS

7-8 cups/1 kg/2 lb carrots, sliced
approx. 3 cups/450 g/1 lb sweet potatoes, sliced
¼ cup/50 g/2 oz brown sugar
15 g/1 tbsp flour
5 g/1 tsp aniseed
½ cup + 2 tbsp/150 g/5 oz butter
oven temperature 200°/400°F/Gas 6

PREPARATION

♦ Cook the carrots and sweet potatoes for about an hour.
♦ Mix together the brown sugar, flour and aniseed.
♦ Melt the butter and pour it into an ovenproof dish, making sure all the surfaces are covered.
♦ Place the vegetables in it and stir in the sugar mixture.
♦ Bake in the oven until golden brown.

Spiced Indian Tea

A pleasant tea mixture for this drink is 2 parts
Darjeeling to 1 part Assam.

INGREDIENTS

2½ cups/550 ml/1 pt water
5 g/1 tsp black tea
a pinch of cardamom, ground
4 cloves, whole
2.5 g/½ tsp anise seed
1¼ cups/275 ml/½ pt milk
10 g/2 tsp brown sugar

PREPARATION

♦ Bring the water to the boil and pour it over the tea.
♦ Add all the spices and leave to brew for 5 minutes.
♦ Strain the tea into the pot and add the warmed milk and sugar.

If you prefer a still spicier, drink, boil the spices in the water for a few moments before pouring it over the tea. Aniseed is very powerful, but dissipates quickly.

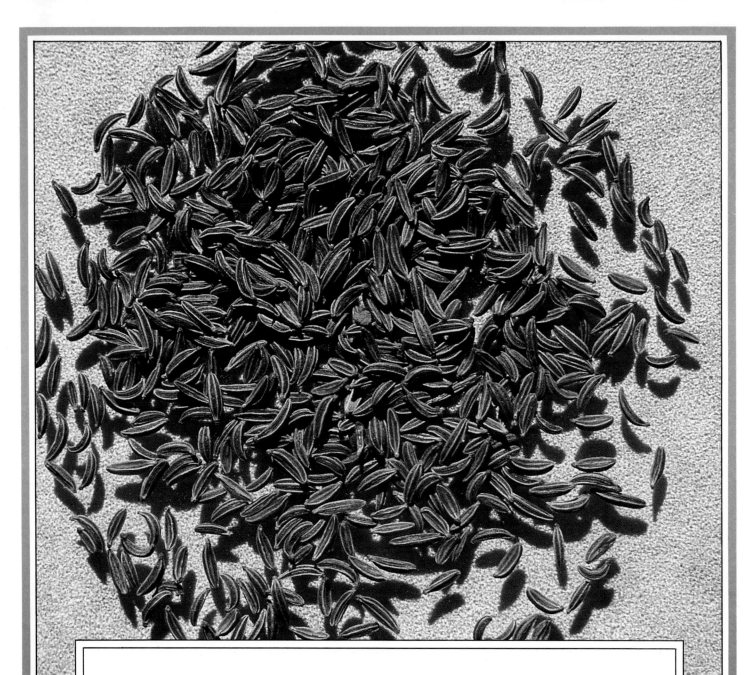

— CARAWAY —

CARAWAY are the little black seeds found in central European rye breads. To some they are the essence of the bread *Kümmelbrot*, to others they merely get in the way. Unfortunately caraway is often confused with another spice, cumin, (is it caraway or cumin the French put in Munster cheese?). To make matters worse, the German word *Kümmel* refers to both spices, but we have it on good authority that the German liqueur Kümmel is made from caraway. In any event, this is a convenient and easy spice to use. Just sprinkle a few seeds into . . . well, almost anything . . . meats, pastries, soups, potatoes . . .

The people of central Europe seem to have a particular affection for caraway. As with aniseed, it has been used as a shield against the effects of the black arts.

Having said all that, the recipes we are presenting for caraway have absolutely nothing to do with central Europe or *Kümmelbrot*.

Singapore is one of the world's great spice crossroads. A substantial portion of the world's pepper passes through her ports. Satay stands abound on her streets. Our recipe comes from a local seller who claims that the secret is in the sauce, and this sauce is something else.

— CARAWAY —

Seed Cake

INGREDIENTS
2 cups/200 g/8 oz plain white (all-purpose) flour
5 g/1 tsp baking powder
10 g/2 tsp caraway seeds
½ cup + 2 tbsp/125 g/5 oz margarine
½ cup/100 g/4 oz sugar
3 eggs
oven temperature 180°C/350°F/Gas 4

PREPARATION

♦ Sieve together the flour, baking powder and caraway seeds.
♦ Cream the margarine and sugar until thick and smooth.
♦ Beat in one egg at a time.
♦ Carefully fold the liquid ingredients into the dry ones. If the mixture is too thick add a little milk.
♦ Pour onto a well-greased baking pan 17.5 cm (7 in) suqare and bake for an hour.

Potato Soup

SERVES 6

INGREDIENTS
6 tbsp/75 g/3 oz butter
1 onion, finely chopped
3⅓ cups/400 g/16 oz potatoes, cubed
1 grated carrot
salt to taste
2.5 g/½ tsp white pepper
5 g/1 tsp caraway seeds
3¼ cups/750 ml/26 oz water
30 g/2 tbsp cream of wheat
3¼ cups/750 ml/26 oz milk
25 g/3 tbsp chopped parsley
½ cup/100 ml/4 oz sour cream

PREPARATION

♦ Melt the butter in a saucepan and brown the onions.
♦ Add the potatoes, carrot, salt, pepper and caraway seeds. Stir until all the ingredients are slightly soft.
♦ Add the water and bring to the boil.
♦ Stir in the cream of wheat and cook over a low heat for 20 minutes, stirring frequently.
♦ Add the milk and parsley and bring to boiling point.
♦ Serve with sour cream.

—Caraway—

Satay Sauce

INGREDIENTS

1 medium onion, chopped
1 cup/150 g/5 oz roasted peanuts
3 cloves garlic, crushed
5 g/1 tsp caraway seeds
10 g/2 tsp coriander seeds
10 g/2 tsp turmeric
$2\frac{1}{2}$ g/$\frac{1}{2}$ tsp cayenne pepper
$\frac{1}{2}$ cup/50 g/2 oz coconut flakes
2 tbsp/30 ml soy sauce
1 tsp/5 ml honey
2 cups/450 ml/$\frac{3}{4}$ pt water

PREPARATION

◆ Blend all the other ingredients with $\frac{1}{4}$ cup/50 ml/2 fl oz of the water.
◆ Put into a saucepan with the remaining water and simmer until the sauce begins to thicken.
◆ Leave to stand for 30 minutes before using.

Meat and vegetables can be marinated in this sauce and then grilled (broiled). It can also be used as a dip.

— CARDAMOM —

*T*HIS spice is a pod about 1-4cm/½-1½in long containing seeds. It can be used whole, including the outer seed container (pericarp), or the seeds can be removed and dried. Cardamoms grow in the lush tropical rain forests of southern India and Sri Lanka where they are harvested mainly through the backbreaking labour of native women. They have now been introduced into Guatemala, which also is an exporter. After the Indians and Sri Lankans — who often use the whole pods in pulses (legumes) — the main users are the Arabs. Cardamom-flavoured coffee is served everywhere in the Middle East. In Scandinavia, they are used in a variety of baked goods and sweetmeats.

The spice is a common ingredient in the ever present Indian spice mix, garam masala. Indians also use the spice to help after-dinner digestion. Along with saffron and vanilla, cardamom is one of the most expensive spices.

— CARDAMOM —

Coconut Cream Toffee

SERVES 30-40

INGREDIENTS
7½ cups/1.5 1/⅓ pt single (cereal) cream
1¾ cups/400 g/16 oz white sugar
1 coconut, ground to a paste
5 g/1 tsp cardamom seeds, ground
2.5 ml/½ tsp rose water

PREPARATION

♦ Mix together the sugar and coconut, gradually add the cream and rose water. Add the cardamom seeds and stir thoroughly.
♦ Cook over a gentle heat in a saucepan until the mixture curls off the sides of the pan.
♦ Press the mixture onto a greased baking tray (cookie sheet) and leave to cool. Score it into squares when it is cool and finish cutting into squares once it is cold.

Spiced Omelette (Omelet)

SERVES 1

INGREDIENTS
2 eggs
4 cardamoms (skinned and ground)
5 g/1 tsp coriander seed, finely crushed
60 g/4 tbsp besan flour
30 g/2 tbsp yoghurt (yogurt)
30 g/1 tbsp ghee (clarified butter)
parsley, chopped (optional)

PREPARATION

♦ Whisk the eggs well.
♦ Add the cardamom, coriander and flour and stir gently.
♦ Add the yoghurt and beat thoroughly. Leave to stand for 30 minutes.
♦ Heat the ghee in a large pan and pour in the egg mixture. Tip the pan so that the egg covers the whole of the bottom of the pan.
♦ Remove the omelette from the pan, sprinkle with chopped parsley and eat immediately.

Honey Milk

INGREDIENTS
1¼ cups/275 ml/½ pt milk
10 ml/2 tsp honey
10 g/2 tsp crushed nuts
a pinch of cardamom powder

PREPARATION

♦ Heat the milk.
♦ Stir in the honey.
♦ Top with crushed nuts and cardamom powder.

Cardamom Coffee

Add 2.5 g/½ tsp cardamom seeds to your coffee while it is brewing. This drink is popular throughout the Middle East.

— C A R D A M O M —

Firnee

INGREDIENTS
½ cup/50 g/2 oz rice flour
2 cups/450 ml/¾ pt milk
⅓ cup/75 g/3 oz sugar, preferably vanilla sugar
1 cardamom pod, coarsely ground
6 almonds
6 pistachio nuts

PREPARATION

♦ Mix the rice flour and sugar to a thin paste with a little of
the milk.
♦ Bring the rest of the milk to the boil.
♦ Remove from the heat and add the rice flour paste.
♦ Cook over a low heat until the mixture thickens.
♦ Flavour with the ground cardamom.
♦ Pour into a dish and decorate with the nuts.

Serve chilled.

— CASSIA —

*I*T CAN be fairly said that one man's cinnamon is another man's cassia. The two spices consist of the inner bark of related species of evergreen. To the British, only the Sri Lankan bark known as *Cinnamomum zeylanicum* can be called cinnamon. The rest are cassia. In America, however, any of the sweet barks may be called cinnamon even though they come from other places than Sri Lanka. In fact, the United States imports virtually none of the spice the British would call cinnamon.

It is unlikely that this can be too limiting because even the French have only one word for the two spices, *cannelle.*

Cinnamomum zeylanicum generally can be recognized by the almost paper thin, but still stiff, components of the stick. Cassia comes either in unrolled lumps or in thicker pieces of stick.

Cinnamon is supposed to be the lighter and more refined in flavour.

Cassia is native to Indonesia, China and Vietnam.

— CASSIA —

Dream Bars

MAKES 15

INGREDIENTS
PART 1
¼ cup/50 g/2 oz brown sugar
½ cup/100 g/4 oz butter
1 cup + 2 tbsp/100 g/4 oz flour
oven temperature 180°C/350°F/Gas 4

PREPARATION

♦ Cream the sugar and butter, then add the sieved flour.
♦ Press into a greased oblong pan 23×32cm (9×13in).
♦ Bake in a preheated oven for about 15 minutes.

INGREDIENTS
PART 2
3 eggs
½ cup/100 g/4 oz brown sugar
¾ cup/75 g/3 oz plain (all-purpose) flour
5 g/1 tsp baking powder
5 g/1 tsp cassia
⅓ cup/50 g/2 oz coconut flakes
¾ cup/75 g/3 oz chopped walnuts
oven temperature 170°C/325°F/Gas 3

PREPARATION

♦ Beat the eggs and add the sugar.
♦ Mix together the flour, baking powder, cassia, coconut flakes and nuts. Beat this into the egg mixture.
♦ Pour the whole mixture onto part 1 and bake again in a preheated oven for 30 minutes.
♦ When cool cut into bars.

Parkin Brownies

MAKES 8-12

INGREDIENTS
1½ cups/150 g/6 oz wholewheat flour
2 cups/150 g/6 oz fine oatmeal
10 g/2 tsp allspice
10 g/2 tsp ginger
10 g/2 tsp cassia
10 g/2 tsp cream of tartar
5 g/1 tsp bicarbonate of soda
½ cup/100 g/4 oz margarine
⅓ cup/75g/3 oz brown sugar
¾ cup/175 ml/6 oz golden syrup (corn syrup)
1 egg, beaten
oven temperature 150°C/300°F/Gas 2

PREPARATION

♦ Mix all the dry ingredients, apart from the brown sugar, together.
♦ Add margarine and mix.
♦ Warm the brown sugar and golden syrup in a separate bowl and stir into the margarine mixture.
♦ Add the egg and mix well.
♦ Pour mixture into a well-greased baking pan and bake for 1-1½ hours.
♦ Turn out onto a clean tray and cut into slices when cool.

Plantain Tarts

INGREDIENTS
PASTRY
2 cups/200 g/8 oz plain (all-purpose) flour
5 g/1 tsp cassia
2.5 g/½ tsp freshly grated nutmeg
salt to taste
½ cup/100 g/4 oz margarine
iced water
FILLING
15 g/1 tbsp butter
1¼ cups/100 g/4 oz plantain, very ripe and mashed
¼ cup/50 g/2 oz brown sugar
2.5 g/½ tsp freshly grated nutmeg
5 ml/1 tsp vanilla essence (extract)
1 tbsp/15 g/½ oz raisins (handful)
oven temperature 230°C/450°F/Gas 8

PREPARATION

♦ Sieve together the flour, cassia and nutmeg and add the salt.
♦ Rub in the margarine until the consistency is that of fine breadcrumbs.
♦ Add sufficient iced water to just hold the mixture together. Leave in a cool place for 2 hours.
♦ To make the filling, melt the butter in a saucepan and add the plantain and brown sugar. Cook thoroughly over a low heat.
♦ Remove the cooked plantains from the heat and add the nutmeg, vanilla and raisins.
♦ Turn the pastry out onto a floured board, roll it out thinly and cut it into 10cm (4in) circles.
♦ Place a large spoonful of the filling in the middle of each circle.
♦ Fold each circle over, pinch the edges together brushing their edges with a little milk or egg yolk to seal. Prick each one with a fork.
♦ Bake in a hot oven for 30 minutes or until the pastry is a delicate brown.

— CASSIA —

Banana Cake

INGREDIENTS·

$\frac{1}{2}$ cup/100 g/4 oz butter or margarine
$\frac{1}{2}$ cup/125 g/5 oz dark soft brown sugar
3 eggs
4 bananas
2 tsp/10 ml ground cassia or cinnamon
1 tsp/5 ml bicarbonate of soda (baking powder)
2 tbsp boiling milk
$1\frac{1}{2}$ cups/150 g/6 oz plain (all-purpose) flour
1 tsp/5 ml baking powder
oven temperature 190°C/375°F/Gas 5

PREPARATION

♦ Melt the butter and sugar together.
♦ Beat in the eggs
♦ Mash the bananas with the cassia or cinnamon. Add to the egg mixture.
♦ Mix the bicarbonate of soda with the boiling milk and add to the mixture.
♦ Stir in the flour and baking powder, sieved together.
♦ Put into a greased 20×20cm (8×8in) square pan and bake in a preheated oven for an hour.

— CAYENNE —

ALL CHILLIES (chilis) are capsicums, but all capsicums are not chillies. The word capsicum comes from the Latin, *capsa*, a box. Indeed, that is what the fruit is, a box full of seeds. There are two family groups of capsicums; *C. anum*, an annual and *C. fruitescens*, a perennial. There is no easy way to tell them apart, but for most culinary problems, this does not matter. Capsicums seem to be related to both the other New World foods, tomatoes and potatoes.

Like everything else in spice lore, it is difficult to make absolute statements concerning these amazing plants. When the Spanish came to America there were already many, many varieties. Since they have now travelled around the world, there are more varieties than one can even imagine. In general, however, the larger the capsicum, the milder; the smaller, the hotter.

The smaller and hotter varieties are often referred to as chillies. Cayenne is usually sold as a powder. Originally it was the dried and powdered version of a small red-hot South American chilli. Today cayenne powder may indeed come from South American chillies or from India or Sri Lanka, or they may be the powdered form of a mixture of different hot chillies. Chilli powder is a blend of hot capsicums powdered with other spices, oregano, garlic and cumin.

— CAYENNE —

Tuna Paté

INGREDIENTS
175 g/7 oz tin (can) tuna fish
1 clove garlic, crushed
2.5 g/½ tsp cayenne
30 ml/2 tbsp fresh lemon juice
¼ cup/50 ml/2 fl oz double (table) cream
1 drop tabasco sauce
freshly chopped parsley
salt and pepper to taste

PREPARATION

♦ Drain the tuna fish.
♦ Mash with all the other ingredients.
♦ Turn into a dish and refrigerate for 3 hours.

— CAYENNE —

Devilled Turkey Legs

SERVES 4

This is a good way to use up left-overs after the big turkey feast.

INGREDIENTS

4 cooked turkey legs or thighs
melted butter or margarine
breadcrumbs, browned
5 g/1 tsp dry English mustard powder
a pinch of ground ginger
salt
black pepper
5 g/1 tsp cayenne pepper

PREPARATION

♦ Chop unsightly bits of bone off legs and thighs. Score the flesh deeply with a sharp knife and brush with melted butter.
♦ Put breadcrumbs in a bowl and mix the rest of the ingredients with them.
♦ Spread the breadcrumb mixture over the turkey pieces and into the scored cuts.
♦ Leave them to stand for an hour.
♦ Cook on a hot greased grill (under a broiler) until crisp and brown.
♦ Serve at once with pats of butter and, perhaps, a piquant sauce.

Tomato Juice

INGREDIENTS

1¼ cups/400 g/16 oz tomatoes
⅔ cup/150 ml/¼ pt water
sugar to taste
2.5 g/½ tsp cayenne pepper
white pepper to taste
salt

PREPARATION

♦ Cut tomatoes into spoon-sized portions and place in a pan with the water and sugar.
♦ Simmer gently for 10-15 minutes until the tomatoes are tender and broken.
♦ Liquidize the tomatoes with water. If too thick, add more water.
♦ Add the cayenne, white pepper and salt.
♦ Chill and serve.

Artichokes with Savoury Rice

INGREDIENTS

2 kg/4½ lb Jerusalem artichokes
juice of 1 lemon
6 tbsp/75 g/3 oz unsalted (sweet) butter
3¼ cups/750 ml/30 fl oz well-flavoured vegetable stock
1 small onion, finely chopped
⅔ cup/150 g/5 oz rice
2.5 g/½ tsp cayenne pepper
⅓ cup/100 g/¼ lb tomatoes, peeled and diced
salt and freshly ground pepper
½ cup/50 g/2 oz finely grated cheddar cheese
parsley, chopped

PREPARATION

♦ Scrape and wash the artichokes.
♦ Cook the artichokes in salted water with the lemon juice for about 30 minutes or until tender and drain well.
♦ Toss the artichokes in a little of the butter. Add some of the stock to them and keep warm.
♦ Melt the remaining butter, fry the onions until soft, add the rice and cayenne pepper. Stir and allow to cook for a few minutes without browning.
♦ Add the rest of the stock and cook gently for 30-40 minutes.
♦ Stir in the tomatoes and cook for a further 5 minutes.
♦ Add the seasoning and cheese.
♦ Press the mixture into a greased ring mould (mold), leave for a few minutes and turn out onto a hot dish.
♦ Place the cooked artichokes in the middle of the dish on the rice. Sprinkle with chopped parsley and serve immediately.

— CHILLI (CHILI) —

CHILLI con carne is said to have been invented by chuck wagon cooks following cattle drives across the Texas plains. With the blazing sun and the ever-present dust and flies, the chilli was essential to make the food edible. Tales exist that the old chuck wagon chefs were not averse to throwing in a rattlesnake or two to really liven things up. Today throughout America those wild and glorious days are celebrated by giant gatherings of chilli fanciers who come together for some friendly and not so friendly cooking competitions.

There are those who maintain that in *true* chilli con carne, beans are *verboten*. There are others who strongly maintain that even the macho art of chilli making must evolve and move with the times.

Many people are reducing their consumption of meat, especially red meat, so a recipe which respects their choice and still packs the old chuck wagon punch must be welcome. The purists may complain, but the beans (French cut) are essential.

— CHILLI (CHILI) —

Chilli ordinaire

Chilli (Chili) Ordinaire (Vegetable)

SERVES 8

INGREDIENTS

6¾ cups/1.5 l/3 pt vegetable stock
½ cup/75 g/3 oz bulgur wheat
2 tbsp/30 ml olive oil
4 cloves garlic, crushed
2 medium onions, chopped
3 carrots, chopped
5 stalks celery, chopped
1 cup/100 g/4 oz French cut beans
3 tomatoes, skinned and chopped
2 green peppers (capsicums)
1-2 fresh red chillis (chilis), chopped and seeded (dried red peppers
will do)
juice of 1 lemon

PREPARATION

♦ Bring half the vegetable stock to the boil.
♦ Add the bulgur wheat, remove from heat, cover and leave
to stand for 15 minutes.
♦ Heat the oil in a large saucepan. Gently cook the garlic
and onions.
♦ Add the vegetable and spices. Cook gently for 10 minutes.
♦ Add the bulgur wheat, lemon juice and the rest of the
stock. Cook for an hour, adding more liquid if necessary.

Chili Crab

SERVES 4

INGREDIENTS

½ cup/100 ml/4 oz sesame oil
4 cups/1 kg/2 lb crab meat
2 eggs, beaten

SAUCE

15 g/1 tbsp sugar
15 g/1 tsp salt
30 ml/2 tsp tomato ketchup

'REMPAH'

2 slices ginger
3 cloves garlic
4 chillis (chilis)

PREPARATION

♦ Heat the oil in a frying pan until very hot.
♦ Stir-fry the crab meat for 2 minutes, then remove.
♦ Add the sugar and salt to the tomato ketchup.
♦ Pound the ginger, garlic and chillis together.
♦ Add the crab meat and sauce to the 'rempah'.
♦ Bring the mixture to the boil over a low heat.
♦ Stir in the beaten eggs and serve immediately.

— CHILLI (CHILI) —

MOLE POBLANO is Mexico's national holiday dish. At the time of the Spanish conquest of that country, a *molli* was any hot-sauced dish made from the many varieties of pungent chillies available. Archaeological evidence suggests that these *mollis* were being prepared thousands of years before the arrival of Columbus. The *Mole Poblano* was an attempt to marry ingredients brought from Europe with those native to the land. The Aztecs of Mexico knew the turkey, chillis, chocolate and peanut. The Spanish brought chicken, almond and cinnamon.

The idea of eating chocolate with chicken may seem strange to some. When the Spanish conquistador, Cortez, arrived in Mexico, chocolate was a delicacy restricted to the aristocracy and priesthood. It is entirely possible that the Aztec emperor Montezuma served Cortez a *molli* made with chocolate. So when you try this dish remember that once it was restricted only to those of noble birth — and the chocolate was specified by the people who invented chocolate.

A genuine *Mole Poblano* requires a number of different chilli varieties not readily available, along with an enormous amount of effort on stone grinders. This simple Mole will evoke the exotic fragrances of Montezuma's time, and you can easily prepare it in your kitchen.

Onion Salad

SERVES 4

INGREDIENTS
4 large onions, finely chopped
1 small hot green chilli (chili), finely chopped
1 slice of fresh ginger, finely chopped
1 tbsp/15 g/½ oz coconut, grated
juice of ½ lemon
salt to taste

PREPARATION

♦ Mix onion and chilli together.
♦ Add chopped ginger, coconut, lemon juice and mix well.

Just what you need to brighten your cold cuts.

— CHILLI (CHILI) —

Simple Mole

INGREDIENTS

1 large chicken, jointed
1 medium onion, coarsely chopped
6 tomatoes, peeled, or 1½ cups/375 g/15 oz tinned (canned)
tomatoes
3 red chillis (chilis), seeded and chopped
2 cloves garlic
30 g/2 tbsp sesame seeds
2½ g/½ tsp coriander seeds
30 g/2 tbsp/ whole almonds
30 g/2 tbsp peanuts
1.5cm/½in cinnamon stick, broken up
2 tbsp/30 ml olive oil
50 g/2 oz plain chocolate

PREPARATION

♦ Put the chicken pieces and onion in a pan. Season and add water to cover. Simmer, covered, for 20 minutes.
♦ Remove the chicken and drain on paper towel. Reserve the stock.
♦ Blend together the cooked onion, tomatoes, chillis and garlic.
♦ Grind the seeds, nuts and cinnamon.
♦ Heat the olive oil in a large, heavy-based saucepan and brown the chicken.
♦ Add the tomato mixture and the ground nut mixture. Cook for 5 minutes.
♦ Add half the chicken stock and the chocolate, broken into pieces. Stir over a low heat until the chocolate is dissolved.
♦ Bring to the boil and simmer until the chicken is cooked, adding more stock if necessary.

— CHILLI (CHILI) —

THE YUCATAN is that southern part of Mexico which sticks out into the gulf of Mexico. It possesses some of the most magnificent ruins of the pre-Columbian American civilizations. Long before the Pyramids or the Great Wall of China, these people had been growing chillis. The spice figured in all their ceremonies and was even used as a punishment. Wayward children were held over burning chillis and forced to inhale the fumes. Anyone who has ever burned chillies in their kitchen by accident knows how devastating that can be.

That the chemistry of each of the pungent spices is different is evident from the ways in which they react with the mouth. Pepper is felt as a tingling at the tip of the tongue. Ginger is perceived most strongly on the sides of the mouth and the back of the tongue. Mustard, due to its unique enzyme action, causes heat throughout the whole mouth. Chillis, even in small concentrations are felt most strongly deep in the throat. Throughout a meal the effect can become cumulative, so although mild at the start, watch out!

If there were a contest to see who grows the strongest chillis, the Japanese and the Ugandans would be hot contenders.

Crisped Shrimps

SERVES 4

INGREDIENTS
3 cups/400 g/1 lb shrimps, the smaller the better
flesh from ¼ coconut
2.5 g/½ tsp coriander powder
5 g/1 tsp chilli (chili) powder
2.5 g/½ tsp pepper
5 g/1 tsp honey

PREPARATION

♦ Rinse and drain the shrimps.
♦ Grate the coconut flesh.
♦ Mix together the grated coconut, the spices and honey and then add the shrimps.
♦ Over a low heat, stir-fry the mixture in a dry pan (without oil) until the shrimps are crispy.

— CHILLI (CHILI) —

Yucatan Soup

SERVES 6

INGREDIENTS

2 medium onions, finely chopped
1½ cups/400 g/1 lb tomatoes, peeled and chopped
6 green chillis (chilis) seeded and chopped
6 cloves garlic, crushed
chopped fresh coriander to taste
9 cups/1½ l/3 pt water
600 g/1 lb 8 oz white fish, filleted and skinned
10 white grapes

PREPARATION

♦ Put vegetables, spices and herbs into a large saucepan.
♦ Add the water and bring to the boil.
♦ Simmer until the onion is tender.
♦ Add the fish and simmer for 10 to 15 minutes.
♦ Add the grapes and continue cooking for 10 minutes.

Serve immediately with warm fresh bread.

—Cinnamon —

Most of the world's true cinnamon originates in Sri Lanka and the method of its harvest has changed little in thousands of years. Cinnamon harvesters work in families, each member being assigned a specific task. Mornings are used for cutting fresh young trees. The branches are brought to a hut called a *wadi*. First the outer bark is removed and the branch scraped with a brass rod. The inner bark is then bruised and removed. It is cut into standard lengths and then rolled, cigar-like, into sticks. The children collect stray scraps to fill out light sticks which along with the rest of the quills, are left to dry on the *wadi* roof. Most likely, the cinnamon stick you use has been harvested by many hands without the aid of any form of mechanization.

One of the world's foremost importers of the spice is Mexico. There cinnamon is used in chocolate. In fact it is not uncommon for Mexicans to stir their hot chocolate drinks with cinnamon sticks.

Cinnamon is also combined with both chocolate and coffee in the now international Italian drink, *Cappucino*. In Scandinavia cinnamon is used to emphasize the warmth of hot, spicy alcoholic Christmas punches. Above all, the most cherished employment of the spice is to bind the sharp tang of sour apples with the sweetness of sugar.

The spice has always been associated with sensuousness, warmth, and even love.

— Cinnamon —

Apple Tart with Cinnamon Sticks

INGREDIENTS

PASTRY
6 tbsp/75 g/3 oz margarine
6 tbsp/150 g/6 oz plain (all-purpose) flour
$\frac{1}{4}$ cup/50 ml/2 fl oz water

FILLING
5 eating (dessert) apples, sliced
2 tbsp/25 g/1 oz butter
22.5 g/1$\frac{1}{2}$ tbsp demerara sugar
7.5-cm/3-in cinnamon stick, broken
1 egg
$\frac{1}{4}$ cup/50 ml/2 fl oz double (table) cream
oven temperature 200°C/400°F/Gas 6

PREPARATION

♦ First make the pastry by rubbing the margarine into the flour, then adding the water to form a ball.
♦ Line a 20-cm/8-in flan dish (pie plate) with the pastry. Cover with a piece of greaseproof (waxed) paper or foil. Fill with baking beans and bake for 20 minutes.
♦ Cook the apples, butter, sugar and cinnamon until the apples are just soft.
♦ Drain the apples, reserving the juice. Lay the apples in the baked pastry case.
♦ Mix together the egg, cream and reserved juice. Pour the mixture over the apples.
♦ Bake for 20 minutes.

— CINNAMON —

Apple Cake

MAKES 8 SLICES

INGREDIENTS
CAKE
2 eggs
⅓ cup/75 g/3 oz sugar
5 ml/1 tsp vanilla essence (extract)
⅓ cup/75 ml/3 fl oz vegetable oil
6 tbsp/150 g/6 oz plain (all-purpose) flour
10 g/2 tsp baking powder
a pinch of salt
45 ml/3 tbsp orange juice
FILLING
6 eating (dessert) apples, peeled, cored and sliced
¼ cup/50 g/2 oz demerara sugar
1 5-cm long quill cinnamon (piece of cinnamon stick) crushed
lemon juice
oven temperature 180°C/350°F/Gas 4

PREPARATION

♦ Beat the eggs, sugar and vanilla together and then beat in the oil.
♦ Sift the flour, baking powder and salt together and fold them into the egg mixture, while adding the orange juice bit by bit.
♦ Spoon half the batter into a well-greased 20cm (8in) square baking tin (pan).
♦ To make the filling, slice the apples finely and mix with the sugar, crushed cinnamon and lemon juice.
♦ Add the apple filling to the batter and cover with the remaining batter.
♦ Bake in the oven for 50-60 minutes.

Sweet Potato Pie

SERVES 4-6
This recipe is from the Caribbean, so sweet potatoes from a West Indian store should be perfect. The yellower sweet potatoes from the Middle East will work just as well.

INGREDIENTS
1 kg/2 lb sweet potatoes
1 egg, beaten
3 tbsp/45 g/1½ oz margarine
¾ cup/150 g/6 oz dark brown sugar
5 g/1 level tsp salt
5 g/1 tsp cinnamon, ground/1 cinnamon quill, crushed
oven temperature 180°C/350°F/Gas 4

PREPARATION

♦ Boil the peeled sweet potatoes until cooked through, in lightly salted water.
♦ Mash the cooked sweet potatoes.
♦ Add the beaten egg and stir well while mixing in all the other ingredients.
♦ Pour the mixture into a greased shallow baking pan.
♦ Bake for an hour.
♦ Cut into serving squares while still warm.

Date Jam

INGREDIENTS
approx. 3 cups/1 kg/2 lb stoned dates
3¼ cups/725 ml/26 fl oz water
4 cups/1 kg/1 lb preserving sugar
5 g/1 tsp cinnamon
5 g/1 tsp nutmeg
grated peel and juice of 1 lemon
25 g/2 tbsp unsalted (sweet) butter

PREPARATION

♦ Bring dates and water to the boil. Simmer gently for 10 minutes.
♦ Add the remaining ingredients and continue to cook, stirring all the time.
♦ When the mixture is thick and smooth, take off the heat.
♦ Put into sterilized, warmed jars and tie down.

— Clove —

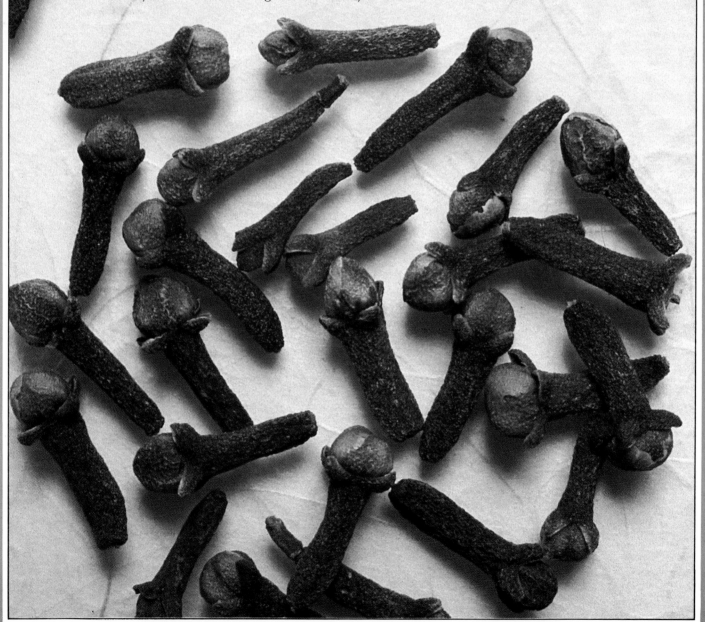

THE WORD clove comes from the Latin for nail. Considering the shape of the spice this is hardly surprising. Cloves are the dried, unopened buds of a type of evergreen found originally only in the Moluccas — the Spice Islands. Over two thousand years ago a Chinese writer claimed that courtiers addressing the Emperor, should hold cloves in their mouths to sweeten their breath. Undoubtedly they discovered that cloves can relieve the pain of toothache. A major constituent is the substance eugenol, which acts as a mild anaesthetic.

Cloves were known in India even before China, but reached the Roman world rather later than pepper or cinnamon.

The Portuguese reached the Spice Islands early in the 16th century, but were ousted a century later by the Dutch. The unwitting natives hoped to enlist the support of the Dutch in fighting the Portuguese. The Dutch sealed off the islands and made it an offence, punishable by death, to remove clove seedlings. The Dutch thus controlled the world supply of the spice for 150 years until the embargo was broken by the French.

— CLOVE —

Gnocchi

SERVES 4-6

INGREDIENTS

3 cloves
1 medium onion
2 bay leaves
parsley stalks (from the chopped parsley)
4½ cups/1 l/1¾ pt milk
⅔ cup/100 g/4 oz semolina
1 cup/100 g/4 oz cheddar cheese, grated
½ cup/50 g/2 oz parmesan cheese, grated
1 tbsp/15 ml fresh parsley, chopped
salt and black pepper to taste
1 egg
matzo meal
sunflower oil for frying

PREPARATION

♦ Stick the cloves into the onion.
♦ Put the onion, bay leaves and parsley stalks into a saucepan with the milk. Heat until almost boiling.
♦ Remove pan from heat and leave to infuse for 20 minutes.
♦ Strain and reheat the milk.
♦ Sprinkle in the semolina, stirring constantly. Cook on a low heat until the mixture is quite thick.
♦ Remove from heat. Stir in the cheeses, chopped parsley, and salt and pepper to taste.
♦ Spread the mixture onto a wetted dinner plate and leave in the fridge for 2 hours.
♦ Cut into 8 pieces and coat with beaten egg and matzo meal.
♦ Deep fry until golden brown.

Serve with a crisp salad.

— CLOVE —

*T*HE NATIVES of the Moluccas, the original home of cloves, enjoyed a mystical relationship with their clove trees. Not only did they provide a living by growing a product which could be sold to the Arab and Indonesian traders, but they were considered as members of the family. A new clove tree would be planted with the birth of every child. Think of the trauma when the Dutch destroyed tens of thousands of trees in order to corner a monopoly on all the world's cloves. Ultimately, the Dutch embargo was broken by a Frenchman with the unlikely but apt name of Pierre Poivre — Peter Pepper!

Cloves now grow in abundance in Zanzibar, which is part of Tanzania, the Malagasy Republic (Madagascar) and the Caribbean island of Granada.

Cloves still grow in the Moluccas which are now part of modern Indonesia, but hardly any of them are eaten. They are smoked in crackling cigarettes the Indonesians call *kretek*.

Baked Ham

INGREDIENTS
1 ham
¾ cup/150 g/6 oz honey
¾ cup/150 g/6 oz brown sugar
3 cloves for each square
oven temperature 170°C/325°F/Gas 3

PREPARATION

♦ Soak the ham for 12 hours in a large bowl, then drain.
♦ Remove surplus fat from the ham and bake it uncovered in the oven for about 20 minutes per 400 g ham.
♦ Half an hour before the ham is ready, remove it from the oven. Using a sharp knife, trim off the rind and score the ham in squares.
♦ Mix the honey and brown sugar and paint the surface of the ham.
♦ Stick a clove into each of the scored squares.
♦ Return the ham to the oven and cook for a further 30 minutes.

Lemon and Clove Cake

INGREDIENTS
½ cup/100 g/4 oz butter
⅓ cup/75 g/3 oz demerara sugar
2 eggs
1¼ cups/125 g/5 oz fine wholewheat flour
5 g/1 tsp baking powder
juice and grated rind of 1 lemon
1.2 g/¼ tsp cloves, powdered
30 g/2 tbsp lemon curd
50 g/2 tbsp granulated sugar
oven temperature 180°C/350°F/Gas 4

PREPARATION
♦ Cream the butter and sugar.
♦ Beat the eggs together.
♦ Sift the flour and baking powder together and mix. Add the beaten egg and lemon rind, mix gradually into the creamed butter and sugar.
♦ Sprinkle the cloves in.
♦ Add the lemon curd and mix thoroughly.
♦ Put the mixture into a greased and floured loaf tin (pan) and bake in the oven for an hour.
♦ Dissolve the sugar in the lemon juice and pour it over the cake when you remove the cake from the oven.
♦ Take the cake out of the tin when it is cool.

Veal Clou de Girofle

SERVES 4

INGREDIENTS
800 g/1¾ lb leftover veal roast
1 black pepper, fresh
2 cups/200 g/8 oz Jarlsberg cheese, grated
10 g/2 tsp French mustard
2 g/⅓ tsp cloves, ground
½ cup/100 ml/4 oz double (heavy) cream
oven temperature 200°C/400°F/Gas 6

PREPARATION

♦ Cut meat into slices ½cm (¼in) thick and place in a well-greased baking pan.
♦ Sprinkle with ground pepper to taste.
♦ Mix cheese, mustard, cloves and double cream.
♦ Spread the mixture evenly over the meat.
♦ Bake for 6 minutes in the oven.
♦ Grill (broil) until golden brown, taking care not to let the meat burn. Serve immediately.

— CLOVE —

Khitichree

INGREDIENTS

½ cup/100 g/4½ oz lentils
4 tbsp/50 g/2 oz ghee or butter
1 medium onion, finely chopped
5 g/1 tsp cumin seeds
5-cm/2-in stick cinnamon
5 cloves
1¼ g/¼ tsp turmeric
2 cardamom pods
1 cup/200 g/8 oz Basmati rice, washed and drained
salt to taste

PREPARATION

♦ Soak the lentils for 30 minutes.
♦ Heat the fat and gently fry the onion. Put to one side.
♦ Add the lentils and spices to the hot fat. Cook for 5 minutes, stirring all the time.
♦ Add the rice. Keep stirring until the rice begins to stick to the pan.
♦ Add enough hot water to cover the rice mixture by about 2.5 cm/1 in. Add salt.
♦ Bring to the boil and simmer until the grains are cooked and the water absorbed.
♦ Turn out into a serving dish and garnish with the fried onion.

— CORIANDER —

*T*HE NAME coriander is derived from the Greek *koros* meaning a bug or bedbug. This refers to the somewhat foetid odour of the plant's unripe fruit, a smell which becomes quite pleasant upon ripening. Coriander is indeed a useful plant, with both its leaves and seeds put to widespread use. The Chinese are not famous for the variety of herbs in their cooking, but they certainly are fond of coriander leaves. So popular are the little green flecks that they have been dubbed 'Chinese lettuce.'

The plant grows widely throughout the world, but only the seeds have any commercial importance. The major exporter of the spice are the Soviet Union, Romania, Bulgaria and Morocco.

It should be noted that throughout the ages, and in widely separated cultures, coriander has gained the reputation as a love potion or aphrodisiac, so watch out!

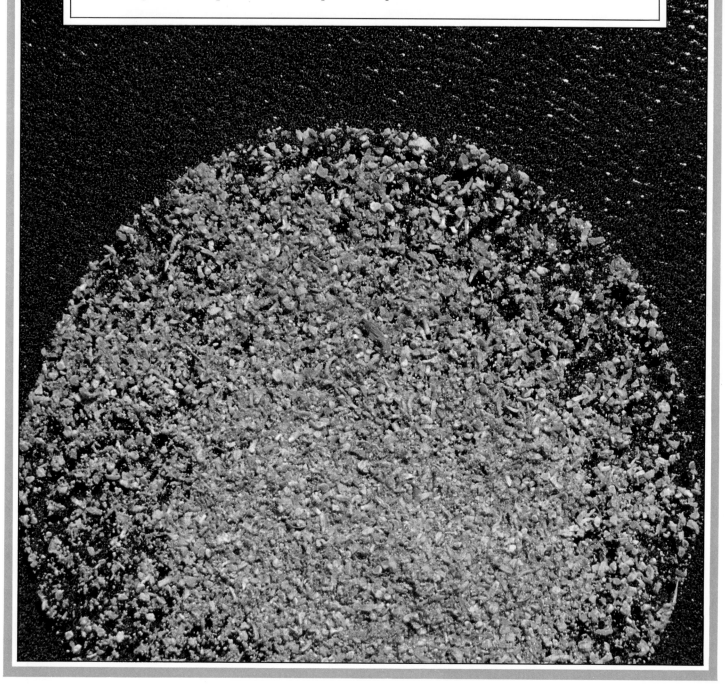

— Coriander —

Fresh Coriander New Potatoes

SERVES 4

INGREDIENTS
1 kg/2¾ lb small new potatoes
4 tbsp/50 g/2 oz butter
4 spring onions (shalots)
1 bunch fresh coriander, finely chopped
salt and pepper to taste

PREPARATION

♦ Boil the potatoes until just tender, drain and keep warm.
♦ Melt the butter in the rinsed saucepan.
♦ Quickly soften the spring onions in the butter, then add the coriander.
♦ Return the potatoes to the saucepan and mix well. Add salt and pepper.

— CORIANDER —

Seekh Kebab

SERVES 4

INGREDIENTS
GARNISH
1 lemon
1 onion
1 tomato
1 egg
2 cups/400 g/1 lb finely minced (ground) beef
5 g/1 tsp coriander seeds, ground
2.5 g/½ tsp chilli (chili) powder
2.5 g/½ tsp cumin
2.5 g/½ tsp Garam Masala (see page 124)
2 cloves garlic, crushed
salt to taste
1 onion, liquidized into a paste
breadcrumbs (optional)
30 ml/2 tbsp oil

PREPARATION

◆ Slice the lemon into rounds removing the pips (seeds).
◆ Slice the onion into rings.
◆ Skin and slice the tomato and set all of these aside.
◆ Mix the lightly beaten egg and beef in a bowl.
◆ Add the spices, salt and liquidized onion to the beef and use breadcrumbs to stiffen and bind the mixture if necessary.
◆ Oil your fingers and the skewers.
◆ Wrap the meat round the skewers in cigar shapes.
◆ Brush the meat with oil and cook under a moderate grill (broiler) until evenly browned.
◆ Serve with the garnish of lemon, onion and tomato.

Masoor Dal

SERVES 4

INGREDIENTS
⅔ cup/150 g/6 oz red lentils
1 medium size onion, finely chopped
2.5 g/½ tsp chilli (chili) powder
5 g/1 tsp coriander seeds, ground
25 g/5 tsp ghee (clarified butter)
5 g/1 tsp zeera (ground cumin)
a pinch of turmeric
coriander leaves, chopped
½ green chili, chopped

PREPARATION

◆ Wash the lentils thoroughly.
◆ Put the lentils, half the onion, the chilli powder and the ground coriander into a large saucepan of water and bring to the boil. Simmer gently until lentils are cooked. Skim the froth off from time to time.
◆ Meanwhile, heat the ghee and fry the other half of the onion with the zeera and turmeric.
◆ Add the fried onion to the lentils, ensuring that the fat does not splutter.
◆ Garnish with coriander leaves and green chilli.

Ratatouille

SERVES 4

INGREDIENTS
5 tomatoes
2 aubergines (eggplant)
salt
1 large green pepper (capsicum)
5 courgettes (zucchini)
45 ml/3 tbsp olive oil
2 onions, chopped
2 cloves garlic, crushed
a drop of tabasco sauce
10 coriander seeds

PREPARATION

◆ Skin and chop the tomatoes.
◆ Cut the aubergines into slices and sprinkle them with salt. Place them in a colander and leave them to drain.
◆ Remove the pith and seeds from the pepper and slice.
◆ Slice the courgettes.
◆ Heat the oil and cook the onions and garlic.
◆ Wash the aubergines and dry them on kitchen paper.
◆ Add all the vegetables and seasoning to the onions and garlic.
◆ Add the tabasco sauce and coriander seeds and cover. Simmer for 40 minutes.

— CORIANDER —

Spicy Bean Salad

SERVES 6

INGREDIENTS
$\frac{1}{3}$ cup/75 ml/3 fl oz olive oil
$1\frac{1}{4}$ tbsp/37 ml/1$\frac{1}{2}$ fl oz wine vinegar
$\frac{1}{4}$ tsp/1$\frac{1}{4}$ ml freshly ground coriander seeds
$\frac{1}{4}$ tsp/1$\frac{1}{4}$ ml freshly ground cumin
$\frac{1}{4}$ tsp/1$\frac{1}{4}$ ml chilli (chili) powder
1 clove garlic, crushed
1 cup/200 g/8 oz cooked red kidney beans
$\frac{1}{2}$ cucumber, peeled and cut into chunks

PREPARATION

♦ Blend the olive oil, vinegar and spices together.
♦ Pour the mixture over warm, freshly cooked kidney beans.
♦ Add the cucumber and combine well.
♦ Let the beans and cucumber marinate in the dressing.
♦ Before serving, drain off any excess liquid.

— Cumin —

*I*NDIAN restaurants have so proliferated in recent years that if a person has not met a Tandoori Chicken, he or she was probably living on the moon. A 'tandoor', you will remember, is a hot, clay, vase-shaped oven with smouldering charcoal in the bottom. A chicken so cooked always seems hot, spicy and deliciously coloured red. For those readers who happen to have tandoors in their kitchens well, good luck. Actually, you might find this tandoori recipe very interesting.

For those of you lacking tandoors (the vast majority, we suspect), you will find the recipe a delight in its own right and very reminiscent of the real thing.

It is perfectly acceptable, and quite common, for Indian cooks to roast fish in their ovens. So, we have chosen a readily available variety that is not only delicious, but works.

This recipe, however, will not turn the fish 'tandoori' red. In fact, we have noticed other tandoor recipes which call upon food colouring to perform this honourable and ancient task. We do not think it really necessary.

It should also be noted that we have eaten in some so-called 'authentic' restaurants which, we are certain, employ the same trick, and also, we suspect, not the tandoor, but the microwave. But that wouldn't be your favourite restaurant, would it?

Cumin is a favourite spice of the Greek, Arab and Turkish cooking which encircles the Mediterranean. It goes especially well with aubergines (eggplant). Cumin, along with the other spices called for by this recipe, should be heated in a frying pan with a bit of oil until aromatic before using.

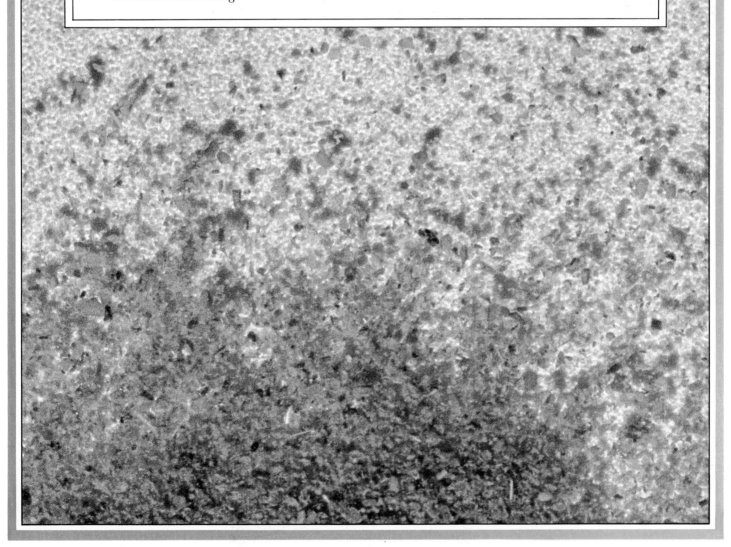

Tandoori Sole

INGREDIENTS

10 g/2 tsp cumin
2½ g/½ tsp turmeric
2½ g/½ tsp cloves
2½ g/½ tsp cardamom seeds
2½ g/½ tsp chilli (chili) powder
2½ g/½ tsp freshly ground black pepper
2½ g/½ tsp yellow mustard seeds
1 medium onion, chopped
2 cloves garlic, finely chopped
1 cup/225 ml/8 oz yoghurt
6 fillets sole, skinned, or any other white fish
oven temperature 180°C/350°F/Gas 4

PREPARATION

◆ Grind the spices together and blend with the onion and garlic.
◆ Mix into the yoghurt.
◆ Marinate the fish in the yoghurt mixture for 6 hours.
◆ Remove the fish from the marinade, wrap in foil and bake for 30 minutes.

VARIATION

This recipe can be used for chicken. Double the amount of yoghurt, marinate for 12 hours and cook for an hour.

— CUMIN —

Felafel

SERVES 4

This is the Israeli version of felafels. The Egyptians make them with dried white broad beans (fava beans) instead of chick peas.

INGREDIENTS

$1\frac{1}{2}$ cups/200 g/8 oz chick peas (garbanzos)
1 large onion, finely chopped
1 clove garlic, crushed
15 g/1 tbsp parsley, finely chopped
5 g/1 tsp cumin
5 g/1 tsp ground coriander
5 g/1 tsp baking powder
salt to taste
cayenne pepper, a pinch
wholewheat flour, to roll mixture in
vegetable oil for frying

PREPARATION

◆ Soak the chick peas overnight in cold water. Drain and rinse thoroughly. Cook in unsalted water for 1 hour or until tender.
◆ Drain the chick peas and pass through a vegetable mill.
◆ Add all the other ingredients and again pass through a vegetable mill. Allow the mixture to stand for $\frac{1}{2}$ hour in the fridge.
◆ Take tablespoons of the mixture and form into small flat cakes. Leave to stand for a further 15 minutes.
◆ Roll in wholewheat flour and fry in hot oil until brown on both sides.

Serve with bread, salads and tahini cream salad.

Tahini Cream Salad

SERVES 4

This recipe can be made in a liquidizer which gives a much smoother paste. By adding $\frac{1}{2}$ cup/100 ml/4 oz yoghurt, which makes a difference to the flavour, a much creamier texture is obtained.

INGREDIENTS

2 cloves garlic
salt to taste
juice 2 lemons
$\frac{2}{3}$ cup/125 ml/$\frac{1}{4}$ pt tahini paste
2.5 g/$\frac{1}{2}$ tsp cumin
30 g/2 tbsp parsley, chopped for garnish

PREPARATION

◆ Crush the garlic in salt and mix with a little lemon juice in a large bowl.
◆ Add tahini paste, mixing well, then add the remaining lemon juice and beat vigorously.
◆ Season with salt and cumin.
◆ If the mixture is too thick add a few drops of water.
◆ Garnish with parsley.

— CUMIN —

Lentil Soup

INGREDIENTS

2 cups/200 g/8 oz red split lentils
6¾ cups/1½ l/2½ pt stock
1 large onion, peeled and chopped
1 stick celery finely chopped
1 carrot chopped
2 tbsp/25 g/1 oz butter
3 slices brown bread, cubed
vegetable oil for frying
4 cloves garlic, crushed
10 g/2 tsp ground cumin
salt, to taste
pepper, freshly ground

PREPARATION

♦ Wash and rinse the lentils several times. Place in a saucepan with the stock, onion, celery and carrot. Bring to the boil and simmer for ½ hour, or until lentils are cooked.
♦ Liquidize the mixture and add the butter.
♦ Fry the bread in oil to make croutons. As it turns golden brown add the crushed garlic.
♦ Reheat the liquidized soup, adding the cumin, salt and pepper. Simmer for a further 5 minutes.
♦ Add the croutons and serve.

Woe unto you, scribes and Pharisees,
hypocrites! For ye pay tithe of mint and
anise and cummin, and have omitted the
weightier matter of the law, judgement, mercy
and faith . . .
Matthew 23:23

WELL, NOT WITHSTANDING that severe condemnation we will leave matter of law, judgement *et cetera* to weightier tomes and talk cumin. Actually, cumin is mentioned rather frequently in the Bible and is a very ancient and noble spice. Its origin has been traced to the Upper Nile valley, but it now grows just about everywhere. The ancient Romans used cumin as a condiment, much as we would pepper today. Medieval Europeans found the spice indispensible, but it is claimed that today's population prefers the less pungent caraway seed. Actually, we believe that the cuisines of medieval Europe and India at the time were rather similar, and it was not until the introduction of cooking stoves into European kitchens that food changed, and so did many ingredients.

The Indians have held more tenaciously to ancient ways and cumin remains as popular there as ever. Quite simply it is indispensible to most curries. In fact, it is one of these ingredients which make curry taste like . . . well, curry!

Babagannouch is neither European nor Indian, but an invention of the Middle East, cumin's first home.

For a bit of a treat, sprinkle some cumin over cottage cheese or in a grilled cheese sandwich.

— Cumin —

Babagannouch

INGREDIENTS
3 aubergines (eggplant)
4 cloves garlic
30 ml/2 tbsp tahini
$2\frac{1}{2}$ g/$\frac{1}{2}$ tsp cumin seeds
$2\frac{1}{2}$ g/$\frac{1}{2}$ tsp chilli (chili) powder
juice of 3 lemons
salt to taste
chopped parsley
olives

PREPARATION

♦ Grill (broil) aubergines until the skin blackens.
♦ Cool slightly and peel off most of the charred skin.
♦ Blend all ingredients.
♦ Garnish with parsley and olives.

Serve warm with pitta bread.

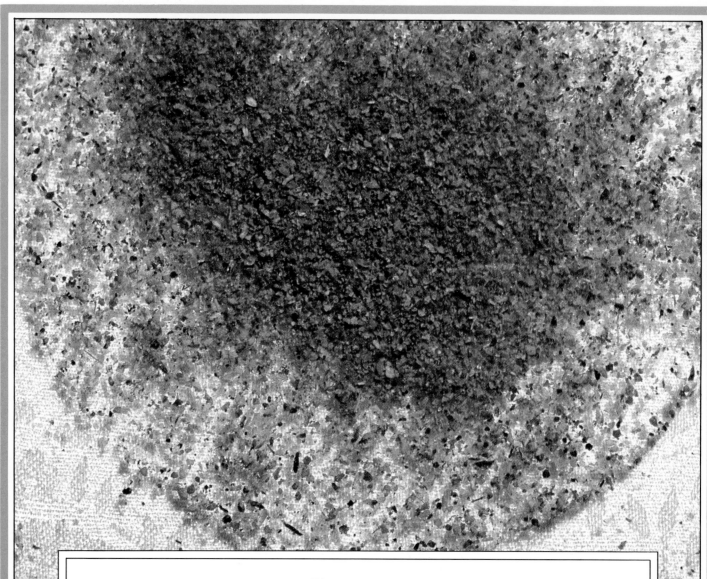

— CURRY —

*T*HE QUESTION of curry's authenticity is one of the great irrelevancies of our time. Curries exist, they have spread worldwide; they are based on the traditions of Indian Cookery; and yes, they probably were invented by Europeans. The word 'curry' is said to derive from the Tamil *keri*, but experts seem to disagree on the meaning. Some say *keri* means marketplace or bazaar, others claim it stands for anything made with yoghurt (yogurt). So much for the experts.

We do know that the British had great problems feeding their native troops in India. The Moslems did not eat pork, while some Hindus ate meat and some were vegetarians. What was needed was an easily adaptable sauce to season the basic rice or bread eaten by the troops. Here was the origin of modern curry, except that in time the sauce rose in importance and took on the name of the dish.

The idea of curry has spread everywhere. Curried goat is the national dish of Jamaica and curried everything is now pretty much a staple of the Japanese diet.

By great experience and trial and error, the combinations of spices and the proportions which are generally considered curry seem to have attained the necessary balance to touch responsive chords, or taste buds, worldwide.

Do grind your own curry powder and do experiment with proportions. It is easy, and it is fun.

— CURRY —

Pork Curry

INGREDIENTS

1 tbsp/15 ml tamarind pulp
¼ cup/50 g/2 oz ghee or oil
2 medium onions, finely sliced
3 cloves garlic, crushed
1 tbsp/15 ml vinegar
400 g/1 lb pork, cut into cubes
3 g/¾ tsp Curry Powder (see page 124)
1 cup/225 ml/8 fl oz water
1 tsp/5 ml salt, or to taste

PREPARATION

♦ Soak the tamarind in half the water for 10 minutes, then squeeze and strain off the juice.
♦ Heat the fat and fry the onions.
♦ Add the tamarind, garlic and vinegar. Fry.
♦ Add the meat and cook until well browned.
♦ Add the curry powder and cook for a further 3 minutes.
♦ Add the water and salt and simmer gently until the pork is tender.

— CURRY —

Chicken Curry

SERVES 4

INGREDIENTS

1 medium size chicken, cut into pieces and skinned
2 cloves garlic, chopped
5 ml/1 tsp turmeric
1 onion, finely chopped
4 bananas, very green if possible
2 slices ginger, finely chopped
2 bay leaves
fresh lemon juice, to taste
2 cups/450 ml/16 oz water
15 g/1 tbsp Curry Powder (see page 124)
cornflour (cornstarch)

PREPARATION

♦ Prick chicken pieces with a fork and rub with a mixture of garlic and turmeric.
♦ Fry half the onion until soft, add the chicken pieces and cook until tender and browned.
♦ Split each banana into two.
♦ Sprinkle the bananas with chopped ginger and fry them in a non-stick pan with one of the bay leaves.
♦ Cover with lemon juice.
♦ Serve the curry sauce separately.

CURRY SAUCE

♦ Fry the rest of the onion. When soft, add the curry powder and cook for 5 minutes, stirring.
♦ Add the water and the other bay leaf.
♦ Cook until the sauce thickens, if necessary adding a little cornflour (cornstarch).

Kalan

SERVES 6

This recipe from south India should be prepared the night before it is served. It is a very wet dish and goes well with rice.

INGREDIENTS

1¾ cups/150 g/6 oz dessicated (shredded) or fresh coconut
4½ cups/900 ml/1½ pt buttermilk
2 large courgettes (zucchini)
½ cup/100 ml/¼ pt water
30 ml/2 tbsp sesame oil
5 g/1 tsp mustard seeds
15 g/1 tbsp minced onion
2.5 g/½ tsp Curry Powder (see page 124)
salt to taste

PREPARATION

♦ Blend coconut and buttermilk together and set aside.
♦ Dice courgettes into 1cm (2½in) squares, salt and leave for 30 minutes.
♦ Wash and drain the courgettes. Cook in water over a low heat, until tender. Remove from heat and drain the water.
♦ Add the buttermilk mixture and bring to the boil. Turn the heat off and leave covered.
♦ Heat the oil in a small covered pan until very hot. Add the mustard seeds and allow them to toast without burning them.
♦ Add the minced onion and curry powder.
♦ Pour this mixture into the pot with the courgettes.

Curried Bean Curd (Tofu) Burgers

SERVES 8

INGREDIENTS

½ onion, finely chopped
1 stalk celery, finely chopped
1 green pepper, finely chopped
1 × 200 g/8 oz fresh bean curd (tofu)
30 g/2 tbsp matzo meal
salt to taste
30 ml/2 tbsp soy sauce
10 g/2 tsp Curry Powder (see page 124)
1 egg, beaten
wheat germ
30 ml/2 tbsp corn oil
oven temperature 160°C/350°F/Gas 4

PREPARATION

♦ Sauté onion, celery and green pepper until soft.
♦ Drain the bean curd in a strainer and mash with a fork.
♦ Stir together with matzo meal, salt and soy sauce.
♦ Add sautéed vegetables, curry powder, and, finally, the egg. Mix together.
♦ Separate the mixture into small burger-size patties and roll them in the wheat germ.
♦ Brown patties in oil in a heated frying pan or bake in the oven for 30 minutes or until brown.

— FENUGREEK —

*I*F YOU HAVE encountered this rather versatile spice, more than likely the occasion was an Indian curry. Fenugreek does have a curry-ish, celery-like bitter taste. As with so many of the spices popular on the subcontinent, fenugreek first was cultivated in the ancient Middle East. Indeed, its name means 'Greek hay' and it was prized by Greeks and Romans alike as both a flavouring and medicine. Fenugreek now readily grows in more temperate climes and is an increasingly popular garden herb. The curry-flavoured leaves can be very bitter, but the sprouts make an excellent salad.

Fenugreek seeds are very small and hard, making grinding very difficult. Mercifully, a small quantity will usually do, but the seeds must be heated before grinding is attempted.

The spice is a member of the pulse (legume) family and boasts a very high protein content. In fact, in East Africa, fenugreek seeds are cooked and eaten as we would beans, and are served especially to expectant mothers.

Finally, in cultures separated widely by distance and time, fenugreek has been employed, if not as a cure for baldness, then as a preventative.

— FENUGREEK —

Parsee Dhansak

INGREDIENTS
1¾ cups/400 g/16 oz lentils
400 g/16 oz lean beef
2 large onions, finely chopped
2 aubergines (eggplant), coarsely chopped
1 green pepper (capsicum), finely chopped
2 potatoes, peeled and coarsely chopped
1¾ cups/400 g/16 oz spinach, washed and chopped
25 g/5 tsp ghee (clarified butter) or butter
5 cloves garlic, crushed
15g/1 tbsp fenugreek seeds
15 g/1 tbsp cumin
5 g/1 tsp chilli (chili)
15 g/1 tbsp coriander seeds
5 g/1 tsp mint
salt

PREPARATION

♦ Wash the lentils and put them into a pan with the beef.
♦ Add the chopped vegetables except the garlic and cover with water.
♦ Bring to the boil and simmer until the vegetables and meat are cooked.
♦ Remove the meat and blend the vegetables and the lentils.
♦ Heat up the ghee or butter and fry the garlic, fenugreek, cumin, chilli, coriander and mint.
♦ Add the lentils and meat, mix well and bring slowly to the boil, add salt to taste.

Serve with rice and onion salad (see page 34).

Chicory and Walnut Salad

SERVES 4

INGREDIENTS
3 heads chicory
1 head celery
3 onions, finely chopped
5 tsp/25 g/1 oz sprouted fenugreek seeds
1 box mustard/cress seedlings
⅓ cup 50 g/2 oz chopped walnuts
⅔ cup/150 ml/¼ pt vinaigrette dressing

PREPARATION

♦ Wash and slice the chicory and the celery.
♦ Mix them with the onions and the other ingredients.
♦ Pour on the vinaigrette at the last moment, toss and serve.

Fenugreek Potatoes

SERVES 4

INGREDIENTS
400 g/1 lb new potatoes
2.5 g/½ tsp turmeric
30 ml/2 tbsp olive oil
a pinch of cayenne
4½ cups/350 g/12 oz fenugreek sprouts (approx 6 oz each)
salt to taste

PREPARATION

♦ Boil the potatoes, unpeeled, until cooked but not soft.
♦ Drain and cool the potatoes and dice coarsely.
♦ Sauté the potatoes and turmeric in the oil.
♦ Add the cayenne, fenugreek and salt. Cover the pan and simmer for 5 minutes.

— FENUGREEK —

Goa Prawn Curry

SERVES 4

INGREDIENTS

2 tbsp/30 ml dessicated (shredded) coconut
8 dried red hot chillis (chilis)
30 g/2 tbsp coriander seeds
20 fenugreek seeds
5 g/1 tsp mustard seeds
8 cloves garlic, crushed
salt to taste
5 g/1 tsp cumin seeds
5 g/1 tsp ground turmeric
5 g/1 tsp fresh ginger
1 medium onion, chopped
4 tbsp/50 g/2 oz ghee or butter
1 cup/250 ml/10 fl oz coconut milk
2 tbsp/30 ml tamarind water (see Pork Curry, page 55)
3 cups/400 g/16 oz prawns (or shrimp)
5 g/1 tsp paprika
5 g/1 tsp Garam Masala (see page 124)

PREPARATION

♦ Soak dessicated coconut in 2 tbsp/30 ml hot water.
♦ Liquidize the coconut, chillis, coriander seeds, fenugreek seeds, mustard seeds, garlic, salt, cumin seeds, turmeric and ginger.
♦ Fry the onion in the fat until translucent.
♦ Add the spice mixture and cook until fragrant, then add the coconut milk and tamarind water. Simmer for 5 minutes.
♦ Add the prawns, paprika and garam masala. Stir until the juice thickens.

— GARAM MASALA —

*I*F YOU HAPPEN to be searching for a fight, engage an Indian cook in a discussion of the relative merits of curry powder and garam masala. You see, in the average Indian home you will probably find no curry powder, but certainly you will encounter garam masala. Curry was a corruption of Indian cuisine to suit the convenience of the Imperial British. Garam masala is as Indian as...well, garam masala. It is a spice mixture whose name means 'the warming spices.' There is no 'correct' garam masala. Indeed, each Indian family grinds its own proportions, and even selection of spices. Also the garam masala of an Indian family can change depending upon the season, the state of health of its members or the foods which are going to be prepared.

Rarely is garam masala the complete spicing for a dish, but it is added near the end of preparation to give it life. Curry powders, on the other hand, contain the hot spices such as chilli (chili) which are used throughout the cooking process.

Some Western cookery writers have claimed that garam masala, although different from curry powder, was the inspiration for curry powder. There are Indian writers who refuse to acknowledge even this.

In preparing garam masala, always heat the spices before grinding and afterwards store in dry, cool and airtight conditions.

— GARAM MASALA —

Samosas

INGREDIENTS
FILLING
4 tbsp/50 g/2 oz ghee (clarified butter) or butter, melted
1 onion, chopped
5 g/1 tsp coriander seeds, ground
5 g/1 tsp fresh root ginger, chopped
2 cups/200 g/½ lb potatoes, boiled and diced but not soft
½ cup/100 g/4 oz peas
5 g/1 tsp Garam Masala (see page 124)
salt to taste
30 ml/2 tbsp water
PASTRY
2¼ cups/200 g/8 oz plain (all-purpose) flour
salt to taste
25 g/5 tsp ghee (clarified butter) or butter, melted
30 ml/4 tbsp yoghurt (yogurt)
vegetable oil for frying

PREPARATION

♦ To make the filling, heat the ghee and fry the onions until they are soft. Then add the coriander and ginger.
♦ Add the potatoes and peas and cook on a low heat for 5 minutes.
♦ Add garam masala and salt to taste and cook until the moisture has evaporated.
♦ To make the pastry, sieve the flour and salt together and add the melted ghee and yoghurt.
♦ Knead into a soft smooth dough, cover with a cloth and leave to stand for 35 minutes.
♦ Knead again and then break the dough up into small round balls.
♦ Roll each ball out on a floured board, making rounds the size of saucers. Cut each round in half.
♦ Moisten the straight edges of the rounds with water and shape them as cones. Place 2 tsp of the filling on each half round, moisten the other edges and seal well.
♦ Deep fry until they are golden.

Koftas

Koftas can be served as an hors d'oeuvre or as a main course with saffron rice and is very good with Curry Sauce (see page 56).

INGREDIENTS
½ green pepper (capsicum) seeded and finely chopped
1 onion, finely chopped
2 cups/400 g/1 lb minced (ground) beef, lamb, chicken or pork
30 ml/2 tbsp yoghurt (yogurt)
30 ml/2 tbsp watercress leaves, chopped
5 g/1 tsp Garam Masala (see page 124)
vegetable oil for deep frying

PREPARATION

♦ Mix all the ingredients together thoroughly.
♦ Form the mixture into small balls the size of walnuts.
♦ Heat the fat very hot and fry the meat balls.

— GARAM MASALA —

Chicken Garam Masala

SERVES 4

INGREDIENTS

1 cup/200 g/8 oz chopped onions
1 tbsp fresh ginger
2 cloves garlic
45 g/3 tbsp ghee (clarified butter) or butter
5 g/1 tsp cumin seeds
5 g/1 tsp ground coriander
5 g/1 tsp turmeric
5 g/1 tsp chilli (chili) powder
5 g/1 tsp salt
½ cup/100 g/4 oz fresh tomatoes, skinned and chopped
1 medium chicken, jointed and skinned
30 g/2 tbsp coriander seeds, chopped
5 g/1 tsp Garam Masala (see page 124)
1¾ cups/500 ml/20 fl oz water

PREPARATION

◊ Liquidize the onion, ginger and garlic to a smooth paste.
◊ Heat the ghee or butter in a heavy-based saucepan. Add the onion mixture. Cook, stirring frequently, until golden brown. Add 1 tbsp/15 ml water to prevent the mixture from sticking to the pan, more if required.
◊ Add the cumin seeds, ground coriander, turmeric, chilli powder and salt. Stir in well.
◊ Add the tomatoes. Cook until the tomatoes are reduced to a pulp. Again, add a little water if the mixture is sticking to the pan.
◊ Gently add the chicken pieces. Cook, still stirring, until the chicken turns golden brown and has absorbed the flavour of the spices.
◊ Add the water to make the sauce.
◊ Cover and cook on a low heat for 35 minutes, or until the chicken is tender. Do not let it fall off the bone.
◊ Sprinkle with the chopped coriander and garam masala. Cover again and cook for a further 10 minutes.

— GARAM MASALA —

Cucumber Raita

INGREDIENTS

1 cucumber, peeled and chopped
5 g/1 tsp salt
$1\frac{1}{2}$ cups/375 ml/15 fl oz plain yoghurt (yogurt)
2 green chillis (chilis), chopped
$2\frac{1}{2}$ g/$\frac{1}{2}$ tsp chilli (chili) powder
$2\frac{1}{2}$ g/$\frac{1}{2}$ tsp Garam Masala (see page 124)

PREPARATION

♦ Sprinkle cucumber with salt and leave for an hour.
♦ Drain the liquid from the cucumber.
♦ Add the cucumber and chillies to the yoghurt.
♦ Put mixture into a dish and sprinkle with chilli powder
and garam masala.

Served chilled.

— Garlic —

*A*LLIUM SATIVUM, garlic . . . Through the past two decades its star has risen faster and higher than any other spice. The seeds of the domestic garlic are sterile. Since the plant is cultivated by taking a clove from its bulb and sticking it in the ground, it is dependent upon human beings and, perhaps, human beings are dependent upon garlic. After all, the Bible tells us that the children of Israel, lost in the desert, begged Moses to take them back to Egypt and slavery for the garlic! If it is the time of the full moon and you hear a bat beating at your window, which spice do you want to be wearing around your neck? Fenugreek? No, garlic!

Today in California, the state which produces 90 per cent of America's garlic, an organization exists for the sole purpose of paying hommage to this great spice. The lovers of the Stinking Rose. Each year at harvest time throughout California and the south of France, garlic festivals proliferate, where growers and 'garlic-heads' meet to eat.

Just a few decades ago garlic was considered a peasant spice. More than just a slight whiff in a dish was trés declassé. Today, in some of the finest restaurants, the word is out 'it is chic to reek!'.

There is a famous American court case (famous, that is, amongst aliophiles, ie garlic-lovers) where a restaurant, noted for its liberal use of the spice, faced closure by angry aliophobic neighbours. The court ruled the odour of garlic, and other cooking smells, beneficial to civilization. And some people consider the Americans to be Philistines . . . Well, the Philistines were also great garlic eaters.

— GARLIC —

Moules in Garlic

SERVES 6

INGREDIENTS
12 cups/1½ kg/3 lb mussels
2 tbsp/30 ml olive oil
1 medium onion, sliced
7 cloves garlic, chopped
4 stalks celery, chopped
1 cup/225 ml/8 fl oz dry white wine
2 tbsp/30 ml parsley, chopped
freshly ground black pepper

PREPARATION

♦ Wash and scrub the mussels. Discard any that are open or cracked.
♦ Heat the oil and fry the onion, garlic and celery.
♦ Add the white wine and parsley.
♦ Turn up the heat and tip in the mussels.
♦ As soon as their shells open, serve with garlic bread.

— GARLIC —

*T*HE WORD 'garlic' comes from two Scandinavian or old Norse words, 'gar' meaning spear and 'leac' a herb. Obviously the reference was to the plant's tall slender stalk which, incidentally, makes it easy to plait (braid). For some reason the spice always has had both mystical and religious significance. In the lore of Islam, when Satan was expelled from the garden of Eden, onions sprung from his right foot and garlic his left, while an ancient Tibetan legend claims that the plant comes from the remnants of the broken body of a fallen god.

We know the ancient Egyptians used garlic to purify their houses. Perhaps garlic does have antiseptic qualities. Prior to the advent of antiseptics, soldiers used to dip bandages in garlic juice to nurse wounds.

Until very recent times people did not distinguish between food and medicine. Another way of putting it is that food was medicine. All of the spices, and of course many herbs, were claimed by people throughout the ages to have various beneficial medicinal properties.

We cannot pass judgement one way or the other, but today the use of garlic for medicinal purposes has a growing array of supporters. In particular, garlic is claimed to be an agent which can help regulate the body's cholesterol, and cholesterol is the gourmet's major drawback.

How perfect the world would be if, now that garlic is so fashionable, people who love eating it could be reassured that the dangers inherent in their passion were mitigated by the passion itself.

Aioli

SERVES 4-5

Aioli is a mayonnaise eaten a lot in Provence and Spain where it is pronounced alioli. It can be served with raw vegetables such as carrots, celery, green peppers (capsicums) and potatoes in their skins, steamed fish, cold meat . . . in fact anything that takes your fancy.
Allow 2 large cloves of garlic per person.

INGREDIENTS
MAKES 1 CUP/275 ML/½ PT
10 large cloves garlic
2 fresh egg yolks, beaten lightly
1¼ cups/250 ml/½ pt olive oil
lemon juice
a pinch of salt
a sprinkle of white pepper

PREPARATION

◆ Peel and crush the garlic, by hand, and reduce to a pulp.
◆ Add the egg yolks and stir the mixture into a smooth paste.
◆ Add the olive oil drop by drop, beating constantly. As the mixture thickens add the oil in greater quantities.
◆ If the aioli is too thick, thin it down with lemon juice.
◆ Add salt and pepper to taste.

Scallops

SERVES 4

Check to see that your scallops have milky white flesh and orange roes. They must be very fresh. Loosen the scallops from their shells with a knife. Cut off and discard the back portion and the head. Wash and carefully drain and dry.

INGREDIENTS
12 small or 8 large scallops
lemon juice
salt and pepper to taste
4 medium cloves garlic, crushed
15 ml/1 tbsp olive oil
wholewheat flour
1-2 eggs

PREPARATION

◆ Prepare scallops as above.
◆ Sprinkle with lemon juice, salt, pepper, garlic and olive oil.
◆ Leave to stand for 30 minutes.
◆ Roll scallops one at a time in flour.
◆ Dip each one in the egg and roll in flour again.
◆ Fry in deep fat until golden brown and crisp.

*Garlic Onion Soup
or Big Sur Soup*

SERVES 6

INGREDIENTS
*vegetable oil for frying
1 large onion, sliced
3 bulbs of garlic, finely chopped
1 tbsp/15 ml plain (all-purpose) flour
½ tsp/2½ ml Dijon mustard
4½ cups/1 l/1¾ pt stock
1 cup/225 ml/8 fl oz dry white wine
salt and pepper to taste
a little butter
6 slices of French bread
6 slices Gruyère cheese, approx 25 g/1 oz each*

PREPARATION

♦ Heat the oil in a saucepan. Add the onions, shortly followed by the garlic. Keep on a low heat.
♦ Stir in the flour.
♦ Add the Dijon mustard, stock and wine. Keep stirring.
♦ Simmer until the onions are soft. Add salt and pepper.
♦ Butter the bread and top each with a slice of cheese.
♦ Pour soup into six individual ovenproof dishes.
♦ Float a slice of bread on each and grill (broil) until cheese is browned and bubbling.

— GARLIC —

Potatoes à la Garlic

SERVES 6

INGREDIENTS
30 cloves garlic
50 g/4 tbsp/2 oz unsalted (sweet) butter, soft
25 g/4 tbsp/1 oz flour
1 cup/250 ml/½ pt milk
salt
white pepper, freshly ground
1 kg/2 lb potatoes
60 ml/4 tbsp double (heavy) cream
parsley, chopped

PREPARATION

♦ Peel the garlic and cook in half the butter in a covered saucepan, over a low heat until tender, about 20 minutes. Do not brown.

♦ Blend in the flour and stir for 1 minute. At the same time boil the milk in a separate saucepan.

♦ Remove the garlic from the heat and add the milk and seasonings. Return to heat and boil, stirring all the time.

♦ Purée the mixture in a blender and then cook for a further 2 minutes.

♦ Peel and slice the potatoes, cook in boiling water and then mash.

♦ Reheat the purée stirring with a wooden spoon. Remove from heat and beat in the rest of the softened butter. Add salt and pepper to taste.

♦ Beat the hot purée into the mashed potatoes and then beat in the cream a little at a time.

♦ Add parsley and seasoning as necessary. Serve immediately.

Serve with pork or sausages.

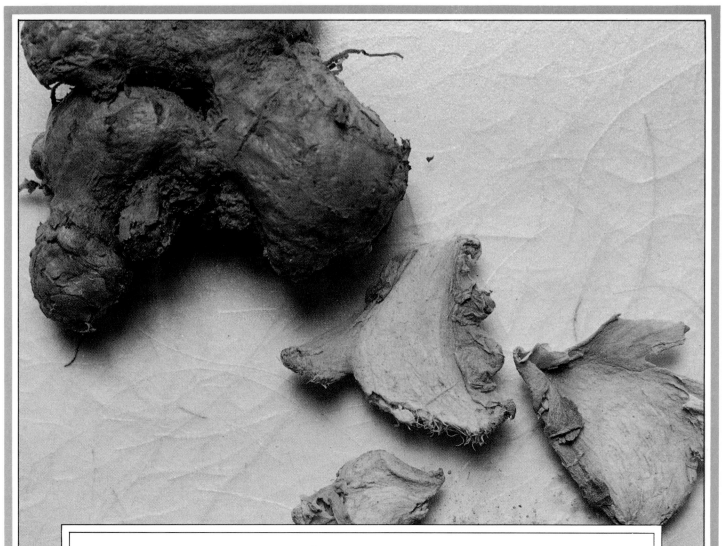

— GINGER —

ODAY you can buy whole ginger rhizomes in virtually any market. Do buy it and use it in the fresh form as ginger has its own special pungency which quickly can be lost by grinding and leaving. If you must have ground ginger, keep it cool, dark, dry and airtight. Ginger is one of the oldest spices, even when compared to other very old spices. In fact, ginger is so ancient that its place of origin is uncertain, but thought to be South-East Asia. Today, the plant does not grow wild but, like garlic, requires human help for its propagation.

It is surprising that so tropical a plant has always enjoyed an abundance in the West, Western Eruope that is, though of course ginger is a mainstay flavouring in Chinese cooking and has been known in the East for as long as anyone has kept records.

The spice was so favoured by the ancient Romans that the authorities treated it as we treat tobacco and alcohol: they taxed it, heavily. The Romans, and the Greeks before them, used ginger in cakes and pastries.

It seems that this particular use of ginger separates East and West. Westerners use the spice in baking while Easterners flavour meat and fish with it. One of the largest and fastest growing uses for ginger is beverages such as ginger ale, beer and wine.

At one time or another, every spice and many herbs have been touted as aphrodisiacs. No doubt this always was to earn someone or other a dinar or a dollar depending upon period or continent. However, the references to ginger have been so many and persistent that it does make one wonder . . .

— GINGER —

Ginger and Rhubarb Fool

INGREDIENTS
2 tbsp/25 g/1 oz butter
400 g/1 lb rhubarb, cut into chunks
2 tbsp/10 ml brown sugar
1 tsp/5 ml ground ginger
½ cup/100 ml/4 fl oz double (table) cream

PREPARATION

♦ Melt the butter in a saucepan.
♦ Add the rhubarb, sugar and ginger.
♦ Simmer until the rhubarb is soft.
♦ Add the cream and liquidize.
♦ Chill and serve.

— GINGER —

Ginger Syrup Sauce

INGREDIENTS

1 cup/250 ml/10 fl oz water
a pinch of ground ginger
15 g/1 tbsp golden syrup (corn syrup)
5 g/1 tsp cornflour (cornstarch)

PREPARATION

♦ Boil the water, slowly adding the ginger and syrup.
♦ Blend cornflour with a little water and work into the mixture to thicken, stirring until smooth. Serve hot or cold.

Orange Ginger Bread

INGREDIENTS

½ cup/100 ml/4 fl oz milk
5 g/1 tsp bicarbonate of soda (baking soda)
30 ml/2 tbsp warm water
2¾ cups/300 g/12 oz plain (all-purpose) flour
5 g/1 tsp cream of tartar
⅓ cup/75 g/3 oz dark brown sugar
½ cup/100 g/4 oz margarine
⅓ cup/100 g/4 oz dark treacle (molasses)
⅓ cup/100 g/4 oz golden syrup (corn syrup)
10 g/2 level tsp cinnamon
10 g/2 level tsp ground ginger
pinch of cayenne pepper
3 eggs beaten
grated rind and juice 1 orange
oven temperature 180°C/350°F/Gas 4

PREPARATION

♦ Heat half the milk to blood heat (body temperature) and mix with bicarbonate of soda and warm water.
♦ Sieve the flour and cream of tartar. Cream together with the sugar and margarine.
♦ Add the treacle and syrup and beat for 1 minute. Stir in the spices.
♦ Gradually add the flour mixture, alternating with the beaten eggs. Beat well.
♦ Stir in the rind and juice of the orange and the bicarbonate of soda mixture.
♦ Give a final thorough mix and turn into a large well greased bread tin (pan).
♦ Bake for approximately an hour.

Melon Cocktail

SERVES 4

INGREDIENTS

1 ripe melon, cubed
½ cup/100 ml/4 oz ginger syrup
15 ml/1 tbsp fresh lemon juice
5 ml/1 tsp kirsch, optional
The ideal measurement is 3 parts of melon
to 1 part of ginger

PREPARATION

♦ Place the melon in a basin and cover with a blend of ginger syrup, lemon juice and kirsch.
♦ Allow to stand for ½ hour until flavours blend.
♦ Chill and serve very cold.

Pine Apple Ade

INGREDIENTS

skin of 1 pineapple
1 fresh ginger root
3 cups/775 ml/1¼ pt water
1 scant cup/200 g/8 oz white sugar
5 ml/1 tsp lime juice

PREPARATION

♦ Wash and remove the skin of the pineapple and set aside in a bowl.
♦ Grate the ginger and add it to the pineapple skin.
♦ Boil the water and pour over the pineapple and ginger. Leave to infuse for 30 minutes.
♦ Strain the liquid and add the sugar and lime juice.
♦ Mix or liquidize thoroughly.
♦ Chill the liquid and serve very cold with ice.

Use the pineapple flesh in a fruit salad.

— GINGER —

Nose, nose, jolly red nose,
Who gave thee this jolly red nose?
Nutmegs and ginger, cinnamon and cloves,
And they gave me this jolly red nose.
Francis Beaumont (1584-1616)

OF ALL EUROPEANS, the English have always been most taken with ginger. Henry VIII ate enormous quantities either for protection against the plague, or simply because he ate enormous quantities. Gingerbread was the passion of the Elizabethan court, even though a pound of the spice cost just slightly more than a sheep. Actually, at that price it was a bargain. Sheep were everywhere, even just outside the palace door, but ginger had to travel all the way from India. Today India is both the spice's largest grower and exporter but it does flourish elsewhere.

The Spanish took rhizomes and planted them in Jamaica as early as 1547. Jamaican ginger is now considered the world's finest. The Portuguese planted the spice down the coast of Africa, so producers now include Sierra Leone, Nigeria and, further afield, Thailand, Taiwan, Australia and China itself.

The removal of the spice's corky outer skin can affect the taste. For example, the peeled light coloured Jamaican ginger is highly aromatic, while the dark wrinkled African varieties generally are more harsh.

The British still, together with the Americans, seem to be the main users of the spice. Saudi Arabia also imports amounts proportionally far in excess of its population size.

Finally, it was long believed in the East that ginger was a protection against tigers. We have some ginger in our cupboard and we haven't seen any tigers for months. It works!

— GINGER —

Spinach Bhaji

INGREDIENTS

800 g/2 lb spinach
4 tbsp/50 g/2 oz ghee (clarified butter) or butter
1 medium onion, sliced
4 dried red chillis (chilis)
5 g/1 tsp cumin seeds
2 tsp/10 g fresh ginger, finely chopped
salt to taste

PREPARATION

♦ Wash the spinach and remove stalks.
♦ Heat the ghee or butter and fry the onions until transparent.
♦ Add the chillis and cumin seeds, and fry for 2 or 3 minutes.
♦ Add the spinach and ginger and cook, covered for 5 minutes.
♦ Add the salt and cook until the liquid is nearly absorbed.
♦ Cover again and cook over a low heat until the spinach is tender.

— HORSERADISH —

AIFORT is the French name for horseradish. In that part of France near the border with Germany a popular horseradish and fresh cream sauce is served with meats.

It is entirely possible that horseradish originated in Germany and spread eastwards. Horseradish is generally used as a root and can be powerful to the point of pain. We say 'generally' because horseradish grows with unbouned abundance in many gardens. The early, large, flat and shiny spring leaves make a magnificent, and quite spicy salad.

The chemical action of the spice is almost identical to that of its close relative, mustard. Water causes an enzyme action and the powerful release of flavour.

The ground root can be used in any number of preparations, usually sauces or condiments. The reason is that, like mustard, horseradish, if cooked loses its pungency.

Commercial preparations are available at the supermarket, but many of the bottled varieties are rather insipid.

Making a sauce by grinding the root and mixing with vinegar or cream is quite easy. Some people like to add a bit of beetroot (beet) juice to colour it red.

Fresh horseradish is sometimes difficult to come by, even in large cities. However, it is always abundantly available in early spring in Jewish neighbourhoods, being the most popular 'bitter herb' used in the Passover ceremony, the *Sedar*.

Omelette (Omelet) with Cheese and Horseradish

SERVES 2

INGREDIENTS
4 eggs
1 tbsp/15 ml water
salt and pepper to taste
a little butter
½ cup/50 g/2 oz grated cheddar cheese
1 tsp/5 ml fresh horseradish, finely chopped or grated

PREPARATION

◆ Mix the eggs, water, salt and pepper.
◆ Heat frying pan and add a touch of butter.
◆ When fairly hot pour in the eggs.
◆ Sprinkle over the cheese and horseradish when the omelette is nearly cooked.

Serve with a tomato salad.

— HORSERADISH —

Horseradish and Apple Sauce

INGREDIENTS
3 Granny Smith apples, peeled and cored
½ cup/100 ml/4 fl oz water
juice of ½ lemon
1 cinnamon quill (piece of cinnamon stick)
¼ cup/50 g/2 oz sugar, granulated
45 g/3 tbsp horseradish, freshly grated

PREPARATION

♦ Cut apples into 8 pieces and place in a saucepan with the water and lemon juice.
♦ Add the cinnamon quill, bring to the boil and simmer until the apples are soft but not mushy.
♦ Add the sugar. Cook the mixture on a medium heat, stirring constantly, until the sugar has dissolved.
♦ Leave to stand for 1 hour and then remove cinnamon stick. Refrigerate until cold.
♦ Before serving stir in the horseradish.

This sauce is delicious with cold pork.

Mayonnaise with Horseradish

INGREDIENTS
3 egg yolks
salt
2.5 g/½ tsp dry mustard
black pepper, freshly ground
1 cup/225 ml/8 fl oz olive oil
5 ml/1 tsp lemon juice or white wine vinegar
45 g/3 tbsp horseradish, freshly grated

PREPARATION

♦ Beat the egg yolks until thick, then beat in the salt, mustard and black pepper.
♦ Add the oil drop by drop, mixing all the time. As the mayonnaise thickens and becomes shiny, the oil may be added in a trickle.
♦ Blend in the lemon juice, or wine vinegar, according to taste.
♦ Add the horseradish.

Horseradish with Beetroot (Beets)

INGREDIENTS
75 g/5 tbsp mashed, uncooked beetroot (beets)
75 g/5 tbsp horseradish, freshly grated
salt
pepper

PREPARATION

♦ Mix the ingredients together.
♦ Refrigerate and cool.

Serve with grilled fish, boiled fish and meat dishes. Keeps for 1 week.

Potato Salad with Horseradish

SERVES 4

INGREDIENTS
1 kg/2 lb potatoes
mayonnaise, horseradish flavoured (see above)
5 ml/1 tsp milk
parsley

PREPARATION

♦ Peel the potatoes and boil in salted water, allow to cool then cut into chunky slices.
♦ If necessary thin the mayonnaise with milk.
♦ Cover the potato slices with mayonnaise, taking care not to break the potatoes, and garnish with parsley.

— MACE —

I must have saffron to colour the Warden
Pies; Mace; dates none, that's out of note;
Nutmegs seven; a race or two of Ginger, but
that I may beg; four pounds of prunes, and as
many raisins as the sun.
A Winter's Tale — William Shakespeare

THROUGH periods of the 17th and 18th centuries the Dutch controlled a world monopoly in both mace and nutmeg. There is a story that Head Office in Amsterdam ordered the governor of the Far Eastern colonies to grow less nutmeg and more mace. Most people probably share the Head Office's ignorance of the fact that mace and nutmeg both are parts of the same plant. The apricot-like fruit of the nutmeg tree is one of nature's great packages. The outer fruity husk is usually discarded but can be made into a sweetmeat.

The central nut, which is the nutmeg, is covered by a hard testa or seed casing which in turn is surrounded by a lovely crimson aril or fleshy lattice. When dried in the sun, this aril turns from crimson to rusty orange and becomes the somewhat exotic spice, mace.

Today, although extensively used in baking, mace is a meat spice. Indeed, it is the preferred flavouring of great French charcuterie, and is found in patés and stuffings of every variety.

If absolutely necessary, nutmeg can be substituted for mace, but do try to find some mace in its whole blade form. This is a beautiful, elegant and very subtle spice whish is well worth knowing better.

— MACE —

Meat Patties

SERVES 4

INGREDIENTS
400 g/16 oz minced (ground) beef
2 eggs
1 medium onion, chopped
1 large clove garlic, finely chopped
a pinch of ground rosemary
1 blade mace, broken between your fingers
a dash of soy sauce
a generous helping of pepper, or Kitchen Pepper
(see page 125) for a spicier flavour
fine matzo meal
vegetable oil for frying

PREPARATION

♦ Mix together all ingredients except for matzo meal and
vegetable oil.
♦ Shape into about a dozen patties.
♦ Coat both sides in matzo meal.
♦ Heat vegetable oil until quite hot.
♦ Cook the patties until brown on both sides.

— MACE —

Mashed Turnips

SERVES 4

INGREDIENTS
1 kg/2 lb small white turnips
1 blade mace
salt
white pepper, freshly ground
2 tbsp/50 g/2 oz butter, unsalted (sweet)
¼ cup/50 ml/2 fl oz cream
parsley, chopped

PREPARATION

♦ Peel and slice the turnips.
♦ Cook the turnips in salted boiling water until they are tender and drain well.
♦ Break the blade of mace up gently between your fingertips.
♦ Liquidize the turnips and add salt, pepper and mace.
♦ Stir in the butter and cream.
♦ Garnish with parsley.

Bread Sauce

INGREDIENTS
2 cloves
1 onion
1 small blade mace
1 cup/25 ml/8 fl oz milk
1 cup/50 g/2 oz fresh breadcrumbs
25 g/2 tbsp butter or margarine
salt and pepper to taste

PREPARATION

♦ Stick the cloves into the onion.
♦ Place the onion with the cloves and blade of mace into the saucepan of milk. Heat gently and bring almost to the boil.
♦ Leave to cool for 30 minutes.
♦ Strain and add the breadcrumbs, butter or margarine and salt and pepper to taste, to the liquid.
♦ Heat gently stirring all the time until smooth. Serve warm.

Smoked Mackerel and Cucumber Sauce

SERVES 4

INGREDIENTS
4 smoked mackeral fillets, fresh

CUCUMBER SAUCE
3 large firm cucumbers
1 large onion
salt, freshly milled
2 cups/450 ml/16 fl oz white wine vinegar
1 cup/225 ml/8 fl oz white wine
2 blades mace
5 g/1 tsp peppercorns
½ nutmeg, grated

PREPARATION

♦ Peel and slice the cucumbers and onion finely and lay them in a shallow dish with a handful of salt. Leave for 12 hours.
♦ Cook the salted cucumber and onion in a preserving pan for 30 minutes.
♦ Strain carefully, removing every drop of liquid.
♦ Add the remaining ingredients to this liquid and bring it to the boil in another saucepan. Simmer for 3 minutes.
♦ Strain the liquid and bottle when cold.
♦ Pour the sauce over the mackerel fillets and serve cold.

— MUSTARD —

FOOD HISTORY was made the day that mustard met the sausage. The great event happened first in ancient Rome, where preparers of food used mustard much as we do today. Ultimately the Roman empire broke into many nations, each of which followed its own mustard-using path. The French use it to bring *joie* to their fabulous sauces. The Germans still dollop it on sausages and the English find it indispensible for making the flavour of their excellent roasts and cheeses untastable. The Chinese and Japanese, who were clever enough never to be part of the Roman Empire, still use it mainly as a tongue-burning dip.

Throughout the ages mustard, which grows easily in temperate climates, has been the most accessible of all the spices to ordinary people. Perhaps this is why it so readily reflects national characteristics.

There are two basic types of mustard seed though botany fans will identify three or four and innumerable sub-classifications, but there are still two basic types, white and brown. The white seeds are larger and more pungent, while the smaller brown seeds tend towards the aromatic.

When the crushed seeds come into contact with water a special enzyme triggers an internal glucoside, causing a great burst of pungency. Most mustard sauces are comprised of crushed or powdered seeds soaked in an acid to retard this chemical action. Indeed, the word 'mustard' comes from two Latin words *mustum* and *ardere. Mustum* is newly fermented grape juice and *ardere* means to burn.

If you take powdered white seeds, add flour to remove the bite and colour to turn the mixture yellow and bathe it all in a bit of vinegar, you end with the yellow menace, American hot dog and hamburger mustard.

Europeans, on the other hand, use only brown seeds in their sauces while, not surprisingly, English mustard is a mixture of both.

— Mustard —

Welsh Rarebit

INGREDIENTS
4 slices bread
4 tbsp/50 g/2 oz butter
1¾ cups/200 g/8 oz cheddar cheese, grated
¼ cup/50 ml/2 fl oz strong ale
2 tsp/10 ml homemade English mustard
salt and pepper to taste

PREPARATION

♦ Toast the bread on both sides.
♦ Melt the butter in a heavy saucepan over a low heat.
♦ Add the cheese and ale, stirring all the time.
♦ Add mustard, salt and pepper.
♦ Spread on toast and grill (broil) until browned and bubbling.

This recipe can be made spicier by using Kitchen Pepper (see page 125).

— MUSTARD —

*I*N EUROPE mustard had been made for aeons in monasteries using wine or vinegar as the acid base. The story goes that a young genius had the inspiration of using the very sour juice of unripened grapes, or verjuice, which was an instant hit. This great event happened in the Burgundian town of Dijon, which everyone now knows is the world's mustard Mecca. Today there are any number of combinations of ingredients which go into the sauces of Dijon and indeed, France itself.

Sometimes seed husks are left in, sometimes they are filtered out. Often other spices are added such as chillies (chilis), pepper or allspice. Even the bases can be entirely verjuice or mixtures of wine and vinegar. People take wine tours of France, but surely a mustard tour could be equally as rewarding for the palate.

But let us not forget Germany. Like the French, they use only brown seeds, but frequently add a bit of honey or sugar.

The mustard powder which has to be mixed with water a half an hour or so before the meal, is still popular in England. Usually it is a mixture of 80 per cent brown and 20 per cent white seeds with a bit of flour and colouring.

Unlike most of the other spices, mustard is big business. Canadians, who are the world's largest exporters, harvest their crop with giant combines.

Mustard was one of the first products to be sold using the techniques of mass marketing. Today, the famous blue and yellow signs of the J. & J. Colman company can be found even in the most remote corners of the world. It was one of the senior Colmans who remarked that he made his fortune 'on what people leave on the sides of their plates.'

When cooking always add mustard near the end, or the aroma will vanish literally into thin air.

French (Green) Bean Salad in Mustard Sauce

SERVES 4

INGREDIENTS
45 ml/3 tbsp olive oil
15 ml/1 tbsp white wine vinegar
5 g/1 tsp turmeric powder
a pinch of chilli (chili) powder
15 g/1 tbsp dry mustard powder
black pepper, freshly ground, to taste
4 cups/400 g/1 lb French (green) beans, cooked

PREPARATION

♦ Stir together olive oil, white wine vinegar and spices.
♦ Toss in the cooked French beans and mix gently.
♦ Chill slightly, but not too much — too long in the refrigerator will dull the flavour.

Devilled Crabmeat

SERVES 2

INGREDIENTS
1 medium size crab, cooked
⅔ cup/150 ml/¼ pt Bechamel Sauce (see page 121)
10 g/2 tsp chutney
10 g/2 tsp mustard (Dijon unsweet)
cayenne pepper
5 ml/1 tsp chilli vinegar
salt to taste
wholewheat breadcrumbs
1 egg yolk (cooked)
oven temperature 190°C/375°F/Gas 5

PREPARATION

♦ Remove meat from crab. Save some claw meat for a garnish and the main shell.
♦ Prepare bechamel sauce and add the chutney, mustard, cayenne pepper, vinegar and salt to taste.
♦ Add the crab meat.
♦ Heat thoroughly, but do not allow to boil.
♦ Clean the crab shell and pour the mixture back into it.
♦ Sprinkle with wholemeal breadcrumbs.
♦ Cook in the over for 15-20 minutes.
♦ Garnish with chopped egg yolk and claw meat and serve immediately.

— MUSTARD —

Russian Salad

INGREDIENTS
1 large potato, peeled
1 small cauliflower
1 piece broccoli
2 medium carrots, diced
1 aubergine (eggplant), diced
1 cup/100 g/4 oz French beans, diced
2 tbsp/30 ml green peas
4 stalks celery, diced
6 spring onions (shallots) finely chopped
1 tbsp/15 ml chives, chopped
½ cup/125 ml/4½ fl oz Mustard Mayonnaise (see page 121)

PREPARATION

♦ Bring the potato to the boil and simmer until just cooked. Drain and dice when cool.

♦ Break the florets (flowerets) off the cauliflower and the broccoli. Cook separately in salted water until crisp-tender.

♦ Cook the carrots, aubergine and beans separately in salted boiling water until crisp-tender.

♦ Cook the peas until just tender.

♦ Drain all vegetables immediately and cool under cold running water, then drain again. It is important to cook each batch separately.

♦ Combine all the vegetables. Add the spring onions, chives and mayonnaise and gently toss.

— NUTMEG —

THE GREAT French gourmet Curnonsky was quoted as remarking about nutmeg: *…anyone who has tasted this spice no longer desires others, just as anyone who has made love with a Chinese woman no longer desires to make love with other women.* You can figure that out for yourself. There was, however, a time during the late 17th and early 18th centuries when the 'civilized' world was seized with a passion for nutmeg. Books were written claiming the spice to be a wonder drug and people carried nutmegs with them everywhere. Around their necks or in their pockets they kept those graters which now fetch high prices in Sotheby's or Christies. A favourite shape was that of a mace . . . Get it?

Nutmeg has been used as a medicine for millenia, a practice which continues in the East. In particular, it was employed to mitigate undesirable side effects of other drugs.

If you are old enough to remember the psychedelic days of hippydom, you might have heard that nutmeg is a mild intoxicant. It is. Myristicin, a constituent of nutmeg, has similar properties to mescaline derived from the peyote cactus. Trying it out is definitely not advised. You will be ill long before feeling even the slightest bit light-headed.

In the realm of folk medicine, nutmeg has a reputation for causing miscarriages. This is strange, since a number of early herbals claim the contrary, that nutmeg is beneficial to those pregnant. Nonetheless, a century or so ago, hospital surgeries seemed flooded with young girls, pregnant, ill and light-headed.

Nutmeg is its own best container. The whole nut holds a number of sentitive essential oils which vanish quickly upon contact with the air, so keep a few whole nutmegs in the kitchen. Graters can be purchased at any reasonable cookware shop, or you can use a cheese grater. Sprinkle it on cakes, desserts, toasted cheese sandwiches, even salads. Remember, nutmeg is essential in all punches and in any number of hot spicy drinks.

Cannelloni

INGREDIENTS

400 g/1 lb fresh spinach
2 cloves garlic, crushed
2 eggs
2⅓ cups/400 g/16 oz ricotta cheese or soft cheese
⅔ cup/100 g/4 oz parmesan cheese, grated
lots of freshly grated nutmeg
(I use about ½ a whole nutmeg)
salt and pepper to taste
1 packet quick cooking cannelloni (approx. 4 tubes per person)
2½ cups/½ l/1 pt Bechamel Sauce (see page 121) or
1¼ cups/250 ml/½ pt Bechamel and 1¼ cups/250 ml/½ pt stock
oven temperature 190°C/375°F/Gas 5

PREPARATION

♦ Wash and cook the spinach. Drain well.
♦ Blend together the spinach, garlic, eggs, ricotta cheese,
half the parmesan, half the nutmeg, salt and pepper.
♦ Fill the cannelloni with this mixture.
♦ Put the filled cannelloni into a well-buttered oven-proof
dish.
♦ Add the rest of the nutmeg to the bechamel or
bechamel/stock sauce. Pour it over the cannelloni.
♦ Sprinkle the remaining parmesan cheese over the top.
♦ Bake for 40 minutes.

— NUTMEG —

Banana Custard

SERVES 6

INGREDIENTS

6 ripe bananas
$\frac{3}{4}$ cup/150 g/6 oz demerara sugar
5 g/1 tsp nutmeg, freshly grated
15 ml/1 tbsp lime juice
$2\frac{1}{2}$ cups/150 g/5 oz fresh breadcrumbs
4 eggs
$3\frac{1}{4}$ cups/750 ml/1$\frac{1}{2}$ pt milk
oven temperature 180°C/350°F/Gas 4

PREPARATION

♦ Peel and mash the bananas, add half the sugar, nutmeg and lime juice, mix together.
♦ Place the mixture in a buttered dish and cover with breadcrumbs.
♦ Beat the eggs and add the remainder of the sugar, beating well.
♦ Warm the milk and pour into the egg mixture, stirring all the time. Pour over the banana and sprinkle nutmeg on top.
♦ Bake in the oven until the custard is set and the top golden brown, approximately 35 minutes.

Orange Punch

INGREDIENTS

$2\frac{1}{2}$ cups/350 ml/1 pt orange juice
$\frac{1}{2}$ cup/100 ml/4 fl oz condensed milk
2.5 g/$\frac{1}{2}$ tsp nutmeg, freshly grated

PREPARATION

♦ Mix together the orange juice and the condensed milk, add the nutmeg.
♦ Serve chilled.

Orange Tropical

INGREDIENTS

$6\frac{3}{4}$ cups/1$\frac{1}{2}$ l/2$\frac{1}{2}$ pt orange juice
pinch of salt
$4\frac{1}{2}$ cups/1 l/1$\frac{3}{4}$ pt condensed milk
nutmeg, freshly ground

PREPARATION

♦ Mix the orange juice and salt together, chill.
♦ Add condensed milk and stir well, add the nutmeg.
♦ Serve immediately with ice.

— Paprika —

THE LARGER varieties of capsicum are more often considered a vegetable than a spice. Often called 'bell peppers,' they are shiny red or green fruits which grace almost any vegetable stand. Paprika is the spice made from capsicums similar to these. As one would expect, it is far milder than either chilli (chili) powder or cayenne. The very best paprika usually comes from Hungary, where it is not just a spice, rather a religion. Usually paprika has a mild flavour and is used more for decoration than taste; but there are varieties which have a bit of bite in them. Hungarians, like the people of India, find it hard to believe that paprika is not native to their land. In fact, it was brought into Hungary by their traditional enemies, the Turks.

The origin of goulash is not dissimilar to that of chilli con carne. The Hungarian word 'gulyas' means cowboy. The dish is cooked in a large pot and eaten by herders at night. The use of veal is an innovation of the possibly more refined Austrians.

By the way, in 1926 the Hungarian chemist Szent Gyorgi first isolated what is now called vitamin C — from paprika! This is somewhat ironic because early sailors on spice voyages were prone to the disease scurvy. Ultimately, the British mariners discovered that this could be prevented by sucking limes. Ever since, British sailors have been known as 'limeys'. We now know that all forms of capsicum peppers are extremely rich in the scurvy preventing agent, vitamin C. Just suppose this fact has been known to early British sailors. They would be called . . . Well, you figure it out.

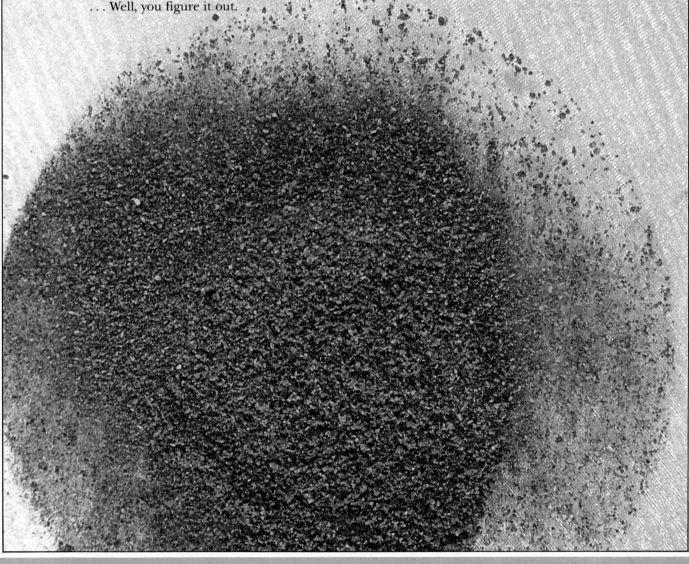

— PAPRIKA —

Veal Goulash

INGREDIENTS
1 large onion, chopped
2 tbsp/30 ml oil
800 g/2 lb veal, cut into cubes
$1\frac{1}{4}$ cups/250 ml/$\frac{1}{2}$ pt stock
salt and pepper to taste
3 tbsp/45 ml Hungarian sweet paprika
1 large green pepper (capsicum), cut into rings
$1\frac{1}{4}$ cups/250 ml/$\frac{1}{2}$ pt sour cream
chopped parsley

PREPARATION

◆ Fry the onion in the oil in a heavy saucepan. Add the veal and sauté until light brown.
◆ Add the stock and salt and pepper. Cook on a low heat for an hour.
◆ Add the paprika and green pepper. Stir. Cook for a further hour.
◆ Stir in the sour cream and cook for 3 minutes.
◆ Garnish with parsley and serve with Poppy Seed Noodles (see page 101).

88

— Paprika —

Fish Cutlets

SERVES 4

INGREDIENTS
*1 kg/2 lb bream (white fish) cutlets
salt and pepper to taste
5 g/1 tsp paprika
2 eggs beaten
2 cups/100 g/4 oz fresh breadcrumbs
vegetable oil for frying*

PREPARATION

♦ Wash and dry the fish, cut lengthwise into pieces, slicing thinly.
♦ Season with salt and pepper, sprinkle with paprika.
♦ Add seasoning and remaining paprika to the breadcrumbs.
♦ Dip each slice of fish into the egg and then the breadcrumbs. Allow to dry.
♦ Heat the oil in a frying pan until almost smoking. Fry the fish until golden brown.

Roast Duck

SERVES 4

INGREDIENTS
*3 kg/6½ lb duck
orange juice
salt and pepper
garlic, mashed
paprika
soy sauce*
oven temperature 170°C/325°F/Gas 3

PREPARATION

♦ Make a paste adding all the ingredients, according to taste.
♦ Spread the paste on the skin of the duck and inside.
♦ Place the duck, breast side up, on a rack in a shallow pan and roast until tender, 2-3½ hours. Pierce the skin frequently to allow fat to escape.
♦ Turn the bird every ½ hour and baste frequently with orange juice.
♦ Before serving place the bird under the grill (broiler) to crisp the skin.

Meat Loaf

SERVES 4-6

INGREDIENTS
*approx. 2½ cups/600 g/1 lb 4 oz minced (ground)
beef, pork or lamb
1 cup/100 g/4 oz onions, sliced
¼ cup/50 ml/2 fl oz water
30 ml/2 tbsp shortening, melted
⅓ cup/50 g/2 oz white rice, boiled
1 carrot, grated
2 cloves garlic, crushed
10 g/2 tsp paprika*
oven temperature 170°C/325°F/Gas 3

PREPARATION

♦ Fry the onions.
♦ Combine all the ingredients together except for the shortening and paprika.
♦ Form the mixture into a loaf and shape.
♦ Melt the shortening in a bread tin (pan) and add the meat, dust with paprika.
♦ Bake in a preheated oven for 1 hour.

— PEPPER, BLACK —

QUITE simply, pepper is the king of spices. It alone occupies that exalted place beside salt on virtually every table in the Western world, but it was not always so. Ginger, cinnamon, nutmeg, mace and even cloves were the great spices of the middle ages. Even the Romans favoured a more aromatic pepper, *Piper longum* or long pepper. Our pepper, black pepper or *Piper nigrum,* rose with the decline of the medieval sweet pot. Cooking in the middle ages happened in a single large pot in the hearth into which were mixed both sweet and savoury ingredients. With the introduction of the cooking stove, savoury dishes stood alone and pepper ascended.

Pepper is a native of the area of India's west coast known as Malabar. This was one of the first regions Europeans found and grabbed after they sailed around Africa late in the 15th century. India is still the world's largest grower of the spice, but the major exporter is Indonesia. Malaysia, Sri Lanka, Kampuchea, and Vietnam are all current producers, while Brazil is the fastest newcomer to the trade.

Since all pepper grows only near the equator in humid conditions close to sea level, harvesting the spice is hot, backbreaking work. Almost certainly today you have eaten at least some pepper and, almost certainly, it was harvested by women with large wicker baskets and no mechanical aids whatsoever.

The word 'pepper' is from the Sanskrit *pippali* meaning berry. Pepper bushes grow about four metres high and are covered with berries which, if allowed to ripen, would turn red. These berries are picked just before ripening and are set out on great platforms to dry in the sun. After about a week and a half, the green berries blacken into the familiar peppercorns we grind into our soups.

— PEPPER, BLACK —

Tomato Salad

INGREDIENTS

6 tomatoes, thickly sliced
freshly ground black pepper (lots!)
3 tbsp/45 ml olive oil
6 peppercorns
freshly chopped herbs to garnish

PREPARATION

♦ Lay tomato slices on a large plate.
♦ Dust liberally with black pepper. Turn the slices over and dust on the other side.
♦ Pour over the olive oil.
♦ Sprinkle with the herbs and decorate with the peppercorns.

— PEPPER, BLACK —

Escoveitched Fish

SERVES 6

The derivation of the name is from the Spanish
'escabeche' meaning pickled. This is a favourite
Jamaican recipe served everywhere on the island ... with
many local variations.

INGREDIENTS
1¼-2 kg/3-4 lb snapper, red mullet or fish of similar texture
20 g/4 tsp black pepper, ground
salt
1¼ cups/275 ml/½ pt vegetable oil
⅔ cup/125 ml/¼ pt vinegar
3 large onions, chopped
1 large green pepper (capsicum), sliced in rings
5 g/1 tsp allspice
5 g/1 tsp whole black peppercorns

PREPARATION

♦ Wash the fish thoroughly, dry and cut into slices of about
100 g/4 oz.
♦ Mix the ground black pepper and salt together and coat
the fish with it.
♦ Heat the oil in a frying pan until it starts to smoke. Fry the
fish quickly on both sides, remove from the pan and set to
one side.
♦ Into the same pan, put the vinegar, chopped onions,
green pepper, allspice and black peppercorns. Slowly bring
to the boil and simmer until the onions are tender.
♦ Allow the mixture to cool. Pour over the fish and leave to
steep. In Jamaica it is customary to leave it over Saturday
night to be served on Sunday morning.

Salmon Loaf

SERVES 4

INGREDIENTS
approx. 2 cups/425 g/15 oz canned salmon
½ onion, finely chopped
1 stalk celery, finely chopped
1 carrot, grated
1 clove garlic, crushed
1½ cups/75 g/3 oz fresh breadcrumbs
black pepper, freshly ground
30 ml/2 tbsp lemon juice
salt to taste
2 eggs, slightly beaten
parsley
oven temperature 180°C/350°F/Gas 4

PREPARATION

♦ Drain the salmon and mash well.
♦ Stir the vegetables, garlic, breadcrumbs, pepper, lemon
juice and salt into the beaten egg and mix.
♦ Add the salmon to the mixture and season.
♦ Turn into a buttered bread tin (pan).
♦ Bake for 45 minutes and serve immediately, sprinkled
with parsley.

Onion Kichlach

SERVES 20-30

INGREDIENTS
4 cups/400 g/16 oz white flour
⅓ cup/50 g/2 oz poppy seeds
10 g/2 tsp baking powder
10 g/2 tsp black pepper
10 g/2 tsp salt
6 large onions, finely chopped
1½ cups/350 ml/12 oz vegetable oil
4 eggs
1 cup/225 ml/8 fl oz water
oven temperature 200°C/400°F/Gas 6

PREPARATION

♦ Mix together all the dry ingredients including the onions.
♦ Make a well in the centre of the mixture and add the oil,
eggs and water. Knead together.
♦ Roll out until about ½ cm (¼ in) thick. Cut into triangles and
puncture the dough with a fork.
♦ Bake on an ungreased baking tray (cookie sheet) for ½
hour or until golden brown.

— PEPPER, GREEN AND RED —

*T*HE BLACK pepper in your grinder was originally unripened berries picked and sun-dried. Some of those unripe green berries are packed or canned in brine and shipped out to the gourmet shops of the world. Actually green peppercorns are most popular in France and especially Germany which boasts an annual consumption of over 500 tons. By contrast, West Germany's annual consumptionof ordinary black pepper exceeds 10,000 tons! The green peppercorns are usually sold in small cans or bottles and are expensive.

Recently the trendy gourmet shops have been invaded by little bottles of pinkish berries called red peppercorns. You can have red peppercorns if the *Piper nigrum* berries are allowed to ripen, but they are not packed and exported.

The gourmet shop red peppercorns are not likely to be peppercorns at all, but the fruit of a South American weed, *Schinus terebinthifolius*. At present this plant seems to be raging as an uninvited guest throughout parts of Florida, the Mediterranean and Africa.

So what, it could be asked, if *Schinus* is not a real peppercorn, especially since it has been reputed to have some medicinal value? The answer is that is has been associated with some mild but still uncomfortable toxicity. It seems amazing that gourmets pay such a high price for a plant which large numbers of people would like to see eradicated from its new habitat.

If you must have a false 'pepper' use good old allspice. It never fails.

Spiced Brisket

SERVES 4

INGREDIENTS
MARINADE
salt, to taste
black pepper, freshly ground
2 tbsp red and green peppercorns
3 garlic cloves, mashed
5 ml/1 tsp soy sauce
5 g/1 tsp paprika
10 g/2 tsp prepared mustard

1 kg/2 lb brisket of beef
1 onion, chopped
1 green pepper (capsicum), chopped
oven temperature 180°C/350°F/Gas 4

PREPARATION

♦ Marinate all the ingredients together, or use a suitable quantity of each to suit individual taste.
♦ Spread the marinade generously over the brisket.
♦ Leave to stand for an hour at room temperature, turning every 15 minutes.
♦ Sauté the diced onion and green pepper until soft and place at the bottom of the pan.
♦ Place the brisket fat side up and baste well with the marinade.
♦ Cover and roast for 2 hours.
♦ Remove the roast and cool slightly until it can be sliced.
♦ Return to the oven and roast for another 20 minutes, until cooked.

Steak au Poive Verte

SERVES 4

INGREDIENTS
4 tbsp/50 g/2 oz butter, unsalted (sweet)
1 full tbsp green peppercorns
15 ml/1 tbsp brandy
sea salt, freshly ground, to taste
4 steaks, 225 g/8 oz each

PREPARATION

♦ Liquidize the butter, peppercorns, brandy and salt until smooth.
♦ Spread the flavoured butter on the steaks and grill (broil) under high heat until cooked.

— Pepper, green and red —

Steak and Stout

INGREDIENTS
800 g/2 lb rump steak
Dijon mustard
vegetable oil for frying
freshly ground black pepper
12 black peppercorns
12 green peppercorns
8 whole allspice
2 cups/100 g/4 oz mushrooms, sliced
1 cup/225 ml/8 fl oz Guinness
1 tsp/5 ml Worcestershire Sauce (see page 120)
oven temperature 180°C/350°F/Gas 4

PREPARATION

♦ Coat the steaks with a thin layer of Dijon mustard and lots of freshly ground pepper.
♦ Fry in oil as for rare steak. Carefully lift out meat and set aside.
♦ Add to the pan juices the peppercorns, allspice and mushrooms. Cook for 2 minutes.
♦ Add the Guinness and cook on a high heat for a minute, then add the Worcestershire sauce.
♦ Lay the steaks in an oven-proof dish and pour over them the Guinness mixture.
♦ Cover dish with foil and bake for an hour.

— PEPPER, WHITE —

*W*HITE PEPPER really is pepper. Instead of picking them while still green the berries are left to ripen slightly until they just start to turn red. They are then sun dried on large mats just as black pepper is. Large sacks are then filled with these dried over-ripe peppercorns and sunk in running streams. For the next few weeks a bacterial process causes the pericarps or outer husks of the peppercorns to separate. Ultimately, the sacks are removed from the streams and the loosened pericarps washed away. To complete the process the berries are placed in large wooden barrels in tanks of water. Bare legged workmen actually enter the barrels and tramp and dance away to remove any remaining husks.

We are told that on some plantations in Brazil this final removal process is performed mechanically, however, the vast majority of the world's white pepper is prepared in this rather harsh and tedious manner.

The food industry prefers white pepper for salad dressing and mayonnaise, where the black specks are undesirable. The aroma of white pepper is very similar to black and may be just a little less sharp or pungent. It is ideal for dishes featuring ingredients which are milder in taste and lighter in colour, like soufflés.

The French often use a mixture of black and white peppercorns called *mignonette*. It is simple to try — just mix whole black and white corns in your grinder.

Spinach and Chick Pea Salad

SERVES 4

INGREDIENTS
¾ cup/175 g/6 oz chick peas (garbanzos)
2 cups/400 g/1 lb spinach, washed
1 tbsp/15 g/½ oz butter
90 ml/6 tbsp olive oil
30 ml/2 tbsp white wine vinegar
freshly ground white pepper
salt to taste
1 onion, cut into rings
½ cup/100 ml/4 fl oz yoghurt (yogurt)
parsley, chopped

PREPARATION

♦ Soak the chick peas in water overnight and then cook them in unsalted water for an hour or until tender.
♦ Cook the spinach in a saucepan with a small amount of butter, but no water. Drain and chop.
♦ Add the chick peas to the cooled spinach.
♦ Mix in the olive oil, vinegar, pepper and salt, taking care not to crush the chick peas. Add the onion rings.
♦ Serve the salad with the yoghurt spooned on top. Sprinkle with parsley.

— PEPPER, WHITE —

Cheese Soufflé

SERVES 6

INGREDIENTS
4 tbsp/50 g/2 oz unsalted butter (sweet)
½ cup/50 g/2 oz plain (all-purpose) flour
1 cup/225 ml/8 fl oz milk
5 eggs, separated
1¼ cups/150 g/5 oz grated cheddar cheese
salt
freshly ground white pepper, a generous amount
cayenne pepper, according to taste, (1¼ g/¼ tsp makes it quite hot)
a pinch of mustard powder
oven temperature 200°C/400°F/Gas 6

PREPARATION

♦ Melt the butter and mix in the flour.
♦ Add the milk and stir until smooth. Remove from the heat when mixture has thickened.
♦ Add the egg yolks, one at a time.
♦ Add the cheese, salt, spices, freshly ground white pepper, cayenne pepper and mustard.
♦ Whisk the egg whites until they stand in peaks.
♦ Stir a little egg white into the cheese mixture to soften, then fold in the rest.
♦ Turn the mixture into a buttered soufflé dish.
♦ Bake in a pre-heated oven for 25 minutes, or until the soufflé is brown and risen.

— PIMENTO —

N SOME spice shops a bottle of ground spice is labelled 'allspice' while the whole berries are called 'pimento.' Shop assistants are unaware that they were one and the same spice. Shame. The whole berries are called for in this chopped liver recipe because they will be ground in the blending or mincing process, releasing the spice's full flavour into the food. In a strange sort of way pimento has contributed at least two words to our modern vocabulary.

The Arawaks were the native peoples living on the island of Jamaica when the Spanish arrived. Unfortunately the whole of the Arawak population either died or was killed off shortly after the European invasion. 'Jamaica' is Arawak for land of wood and water. The natives used pimento in the process of curing the meat of animals and, on occasion, of their enemies. This pimento-cured meat was called *boucan* and was adopted by the pirates who used the island as a base to raid shipping in the Caribbean. Ultimately, the pirates took their name from the meat, *boucan*. They were called *boucaniers* which became 'buccaneers.'

A famous Jamaican treat served to delighted tourists is jerk pork, or pork cooked in the Arawak style. Of course the meat is spiced with pimento, but it is roasted on an open wooden platform constructed from pimento branches. The Arawak name for the structure was a 'barbeque'.

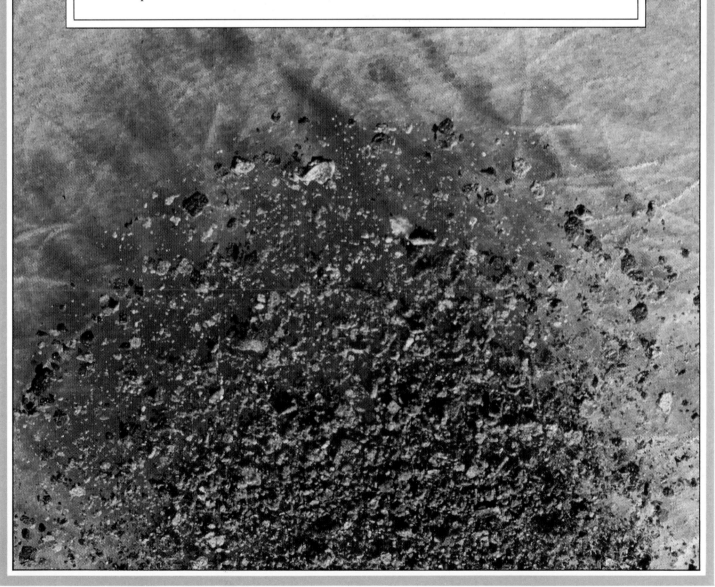

— PIMENTO —

Chopped Liver

INGREDIENTS

800 g/2 lb lambs liver
plain (all-purpose) flour
2 medium onions, sliced
18 peppercorns
8 pimento berries
salt to taste
4 tbsp/50 g/2 oz shortening
2.5 cm/1½ in white radish

PREPARATION

♦ Dip the liver in flour and fry with one of the onions in shortening over a medium heat until cooked.
♦ Cut liver into small pieces.
♦ Use your electric blender to blend all the ingredients, including the other onion, and any shortening left in the pan.

Serve garnished with lettuce and parsley.

Note: If you have an old fashioned mincer (meat grinder) it gives a better texture.

— PIMENTO —

Brown Fish Stew

SERVES 2

INGREDIENTS

1 snapper, small red mullet or jackfish
vegetable oil for frying
2 onions, sliced
5 g/1 tsp pimento corns (pimentos)
1¼ cups/275 ml/½ pt water
7 g/1½ tsp dark brown sugar
tomato ketchup (optional)
salt and pepper to taste

PREPARATION

♦ Wash and dry the fish.
♦ Heat the oil and lightly fry the fish. Set to one side.
♦ Fry the onions, add pimento corns and stir.
♦ Add the water and brown sugar. Stir and make into a brown sauce, adding ketchup and salt and pepper to taste.
♦ Put the fish into a deep pan. Pour on the sauce. Cover and simmer for 15 minutes, turning the fish while it cooks.

Spiced Brisket of Beef

SERVES 6

INGREDIENTS

1.5 kg/3 lb brisket beef
8 rashers (strips) bacon
2 onions, coarsely chopped
2 cloves
1 blade mace
15 g/1 tbsp pimento
6 black peppercorns
water to cover
oven temperature 170°C/325°F/Gas 3

PREPARATION

♦ Clean and dry the meat, trimming off excess fat if necessary.
♦ Cover the bottom of a casserole dish with 4 rashers of bacon and the onion.
♦ Place the meat on the bacon and onion and lay the remaining rashers of bacon on top. Add the spices and water, so that the meat is nearly covered.
♦ Cover the casserole and cook in a slow oven for 3 hours or until tender.

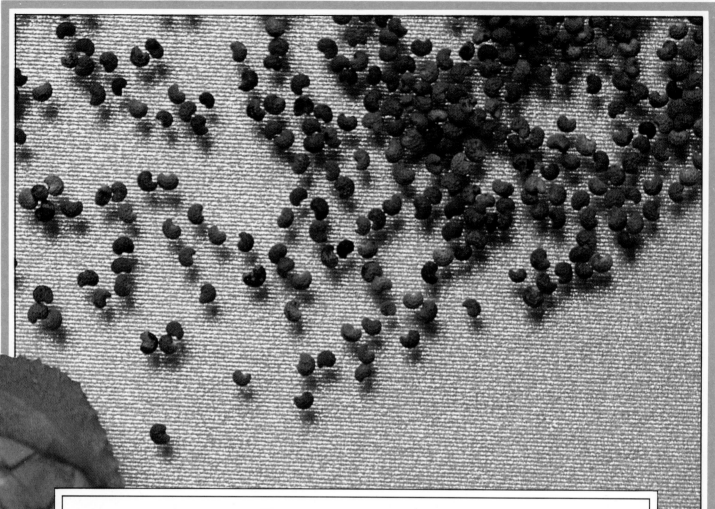

— POPPY SEED —

$\mathcal{I}$F YOU HAVE wondered whether poppy seeds come from the same plant as opium, they do. The white poppy has been at the same time one of the most beneficial and controversial of all plants. The seeds grow in pods actually surrounded by the milky white juice from which the narcotic is derived, however, the seeds themselves possess no psychoactive qualities. The white poppy originated in Asia Minor and is now cultivated throughout the semi-tropical world.

It is hardly surprising that the plant was one of the earliest to be cherished by human beings, and that the tiny black seeds came to be appreciated very long ago. They were a favourite condiment of ancient Egypt and were so admired by the ancient Greeks that poppies were grown for their seeds alone. Small cakes of seed and honey were eaten by ancient olympic athletes to provide extra bursts of energy. The Romans sprinkled the seeds on a type of mushroom-shaped bread, a practice which Europeans have continued to the present day.

The Jewish holiday, *purim*, celebrates the thwarting of a planned massacre of the Jews of Persia and the downfall of the evil chamberlain, Haman. Either Haman's hat, his purse or his ears were triangular and in commemoration three-cornered pastries called *Hamantaschen* are eaten. The favourite filling for these is poppy seeds.

In India, the seeds are used in spicy sauces both to contribute their own flavour and add texture.

It seems strange, but noodles were unknown in Italy and the rest of Europe until the late middle ages. It is thought that they originated in China or Southeast Asia, lands long associated with the poppy.

— Poppy seed —

Poppy Seed Noodles

SERVES 6

INGREDIENTS
12 oz ribbon noodles
3 tbsp/50 g/2 oz butter, unsalted (sweet)
30 ml/2 tbsp poppy seeds
salt and pepper to taste

PREPARATION

♦ Cook noodles and drain.
♦ Melt the butter. Add the poppy seeds, salt and pepper.
♦ Add the noodles and stir with wooden spoon.

Serve with Veal Goulash (see page 88).

— POPPY SEED —

Hamantaschen

SERVES 24

These are traditional cakes eaten during the Jewish holiday of *purim*. Their triangular shape is reminiscent of the villain Haman's ears or hat, depending on which traditional tale one knows.

INGREDIENTS
KÜCHEN DOUGH
$12\frac{1}{2}$ g/$2\frac{1}{2}$ tsp yeast
$\frac{1}{4}$ cup/50 g/2 oz sugar
50 g/4 tbsp butter or margarine
$\frac{2}{3}$ cup/150 ml/$\frac{1}{4}$ pt milk
$3\frac{3}{4}$ cups/400 g/16 oz plain (all-purpose) flour
salt to taste
1 egg
honey
POPPY SEED FILLING
$\frac{1}{2}$ cup/100 g/4 oz poppy seeds, ground
$1\frac{1}{4}$ cups/275 ml/$\frac{1}{2}$ pt milk
50 g/4 tbsp butter
$\frac{1}{3}$ cup/50 g/2 oz chopped nuts
30 ml/2 tbsp molasses
oven temperature 180°C/350°F/Gas 4

PREPARATION

♦ Cream the yeast with 1 tbsp of sugar in a warm bowl.
♦ Melt the butter or margarine, pour into the milk and stir. Add the creamed sugar and yeast.
♦ Sieve the flour and salt together and place in a bowl, leaving a well in the middle. Pour in the liquid mixture.
♦ Work the liquid into the flour, making a pliable dough.
♦ Cover with a cloth and set aside in a warm place for 2 hours.
♦ Add remaining sugar, a well-beaten egg and knead well.
♦ Cover again with the cloth and leave as before for a further 2 hours when the dough will be ready to use.
♦ To make the filling, place all the ingredients together in a saucepan and cook over a low heat until thick, skimming frequently. Leave to cool.
♦ Roll out the dough to $\frac{1}{2}$ cm ($\frac{1}{4}$ in) thickness.
♦ Cut into 10 cm (4 in) rounds and brush with melted butter.
♦ Place 1 tsp of the filling in the centre of each round.
♦ Fold the edges to form three-cornered cakes.
♦ Brush tops with warm melted honey.
♦ Leave in a warm place until the cakes rise to double their original size.
♦ Bake until golden brown.

Poppy Seed Crunch

MAKES 8 SQUARES

INGREDIENTS
45 g/3 tbsp butter, unsalted (sweet)
$\frac{1}{3}$ cup/75 g/3 oz white sugar
2 eggs, separated
5 ml/1 tsp vanilla essence (extract)
$1\frac{1}{4}$ cups/150 g/6 oz plain (all-purpose) flour
7.5 g/$1\frac{1}{2}$ tsp baking powder
$\frac{1}{2}$ cup/100 g/4 oz brown sugar
$\frac{1}{3}$ cup/100 g/4 oz poppy seeds, ground
oven temperature 170°C/325°F/Gas 3

PREPARATION

♦ Cream the butter and the sugar, mix in the egg yolks, one at a time, and add the vanilla.
♦ Sift together the flour and baking powder, fold into the mixture.
♦ Place the mixture in a 20 cm (8 in) greased, square pan. The mixture should still be quite loose.
♦ Beat the egg whites until stiff, then beat in the brown sugar and fold in the poppy seed.
♦ Spread over the dough and bake in the oven for 25 minutes or until delicately browned.
♦ Cool and cut into squares.

— SAFFRON —

*S*AFFRON is the aristocrat amongst spices; its aroma is subtle, its colour is gold, and it is expensive. The spice originated in the southern part of what is now modern Turkey and was well known throughout the Eastern Mediterranean. Today its principal areas of cultivation are Iran, Kashmir and, especially, Spain. Saffron is the stigmas, or female sex organs, of a lovely violet crocus, not unlike the typical garden variety, except it blooms in the autumn. It is cultivated mainly on the rocky hillsides of La Mancha — Don Quixote's Spain. During the two or three short weeks of autumn blooming, whole families take to the field and spend the long, hot days in a perpetual stoop, gathering thousands upon thousands of the lovely blossoms. Through the cold nights, the families huddle together separating the stigmas from the pretty, but useless, petals — one by one — all by hand. After drying, a whole field could yield but a handful of the spice.

Saffron was known in Spain in ancient times, but the tradition of modern cultivation was started by the Arabs around the year AD 900. The Arabs also first planted the rice which grows in the Spanish lakes. So it was about a thousand years ago that the ingredients came together for one of the most glorious of Spain's traditional dishes, *paella.*

Saffron spread throughout Europe and became one of the principal medieval spices. It was cultivated in Germany and in Britain at Saffron Walden in Essex. French saffron is used in the preparation of the best of all Marseillais dishes, *bouillabaisse.*

The arrival of eastern spices meant the end of saffron cultivation throughout Europe, except on those rocky plateaus of La Mancha.

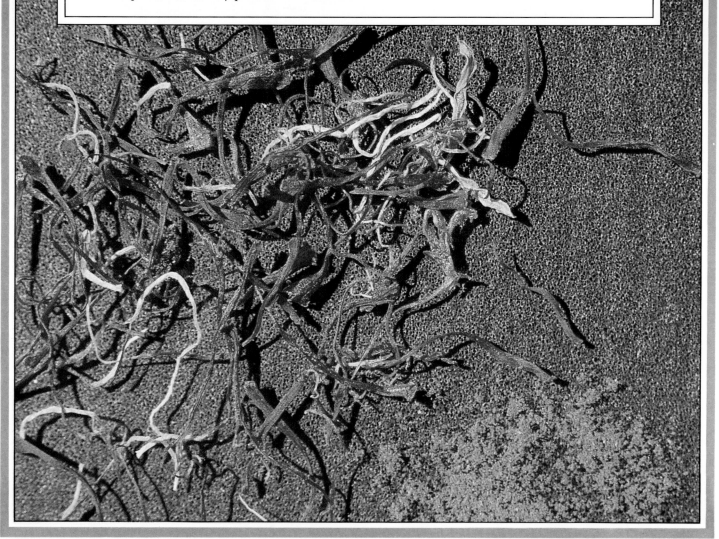

— SAFFRON —

Paella

SERVES 6-8

INGREDIENTS

½ cup/50 g/2 oz parsley, chopped
8 cloves garlic, crushed
2 tsp oregano
salt and pepper
1 chicken, jointed and skinned
plain (all-purpose) flour
vegetable oil for frying
1 onion, sliced
saffron threads, a generous pinch
1½ cups/375 ml/¾ pt chicken stock
1 cup/200 g/8 oz rice
1 cup/200 ml/8 fl oz white wine
1½ cups/375 g/15 oz tinned (canned) tomatoes
2 tbsp/25 g/1 oz butter
800 g/1¾ lb raw squid, chopped
4 cups/400 g/1 lb mussels, fresh, frozen or canned
4 cups/400 g/1 lb fresh clams (peeled frozen prawns (or shrimp),
or cockles can be substituted)

PREPARATION

◆ Mash together the parsley, half the garlic, the oregano, salt and pepper.
◆ Marinade the chicken pieces in this mixture for 2 hours.
◆ Dip them in flour and fry in oil until half cooked. Put them to one side.
◆ In a paella pan fry the onion and the remaining cloves of garlic.
◆ Infuse the saffron in a little of the chicken stock for 10 minutes.
◆ Add the chicken to the pan, together with the rice, white wine, tomatoes, saffron stock, remaining chicken stock and butter.
◆ Stir well and cover for 2 minutes.
◆ Add the seafood, arranging it in concentric circles.
◆ Cover and simmer for 20-30 minutes. Check the rice is cooked.
◆ Allow to stand for 3-4 minutes before serving.

— SAFFRON —

RIENDS of ours returned from Spain beaming and bearing us a large sack of yellow spice which they proclaimed was saffron. We hid our disappointment but had to tell them that what they had purchased was not saffron, but turmeric. To have come by so much saffron they would have had to trade their new car! While we were touring a Middle Eastern spice market we came across a stall piled high with tiny orangey flowers labelled 'saffron.' Although the merchant swore up and down that his saffron was genuine, it was not saffron at all, but safflower, a totally different and less desirable substance.

For centuries, perhaps millennia, people have used either pure saffron adulterated with cheaper substances or sold the latter as the real thing. In 15th-century Germany there was a special tribunal, the *Safranschau*, charged with eradicating such evil practices. The penalty for conviction was instant death. Unfortunately, today's penalties, if any, are far less harsh; however, the chances of the proverbial 'rip off' are still high.

Even if you buy the actual stigmas, it still is possible to be cheated. Taking spent spice and infusing it with yellow food colouring has been known, so buy from a reputable spice dealer and be careful of 'special offers' — they may not be the bargains they seem.

Saffron is used widely in up-market Indian cooking and in many festival foods in Iran. Two interesting pockets of saffron culture still remain from long ago. The people of Cornwall in the south-west corner of England claim that the spice was brought there first by the ancient Phoenicians. Today they still bake their famous saffron buns and cakes.

The other group are the Dutch of Pennsylvania who emigrated to the United States from Germany. Saffron is essential to their famous *Schwenkfelder* cake.

Easter Biscuit (Cookies)

INGREDIENTS
generous ½ cup/50 g/2 oz plain (all-purpose) flour
a pinch of salt
⅓ cup/50 g/2 oz currants
6 tbsp/75 g/3 oz butter, unsalted (sweet)
⅓ cup/75 g/3 oz sugar
1 egg yolk, lightly beaten
a pinch of saffron, soaked overnight in 5 ml/1 tsp milk
oven temperature 190°C/375°F/Gas 5

PREPARATION

♦ Sieve flour with a pinch of salt.
♦ Wash currants and add to flour.
♦ Cream the butter and sugar together until smooth and light in colour.
♦ Add beaten egg yolk plus a small amount of flour.
♦ Add saffron.
♦ Mix and knead into a firm but soft dough.
♦ Roll out dough to a thickness of 1 cm (½ in) and cut into rounds.
♦ Bake for 10 minutes or until lightly browned.

Risotto

SERVES 4

INGREDIENTS
4 tbsp/50 g/2 oz butter, unsalted (sweet)
2 medium size onions, finely diced
1½ cups/300 g/12 oz Piedmont rice
½ cup/100 ml/4 fl oz dry white wine
7½-10 cups/1½-2 l/3¾ pt chicken stock
a pinch of saffron
⅓ cup/50 g/2 oz parmesan cheese

PREPARATION

♦ Melt half the butter and fry the onions until soft.
♦ Wash the rice and add it to the onions. Cook the rice until the grains become transparent but not brown.
♦ Pour in the wine and stir well.
♦ When the wine has evaporated, start adding the chicken stock, a small amount at a time until the stock is absorbed, and the rice is cooked. The rice should be soft and creamy. Stir all the time to make sure that the rice does not stick to the pan.
♦ Meanwhile take a few strands of saffron and steep them in a small amount of water.
♦ Drain, add the saffron, the rest of the butter and the parmesan cheese and stir. Serve immediately.

— SAFFRON —

Saffron rice

Saffron Rice

INGREDIENTS
1¼ cups/300 g/10 oz Basmati rice
1 tsp/5 ml saffron threads
6 tbsp/75 g/3 oz ghee (clarified butter) or butter
1 stick of cinnamon
4 whole cloves
½ cup/100 g/4 oz chopped onion
7.5 g/1½ tsp salt
125 mg/¼ tsp cardamom seeds

PREPARATION

♦ Wash the rice and drain.
♦ Place the saffron in a bowl. Pour on 2 tbsp/30 ml boiling water. Leave to infuse for 10 minutes.
♦ Heat the ghee or butter in a large pan. Add the cinnamon and cloves, followed by onions. Cook until the onions are golden brown, stirring all the time.
♦ Add the rice and stir for about 5 minutes, or until all the liquid has evaporated.
♦ Add enough water to cover the rice by about 2.5 cm/1 in. Add the salt and cardamom seeds. Bring to the boil over a high heat, stirring all the time.
♦ Add the saffron and its water. Stir gently.
♦ Cover the pan and cook on a low heat for about 25 minutes, or until the rice has absorbed all the liquid.

Rice with Saffron

INGREDIENTS
2 cups/400 g/1 lb patna rice
¼ tsp/125 mg saffron
salt to taste

PREPARATION

♦ Put the rice, saffron and salt in a saucepan.
♦ Cover with water to a depth of 2.5 cm/1 in above the rice.
♦ Bring to the boil. Cover and simmer until the water has been absorbed.
♦ Leave to stand for 5 minutes before serving.

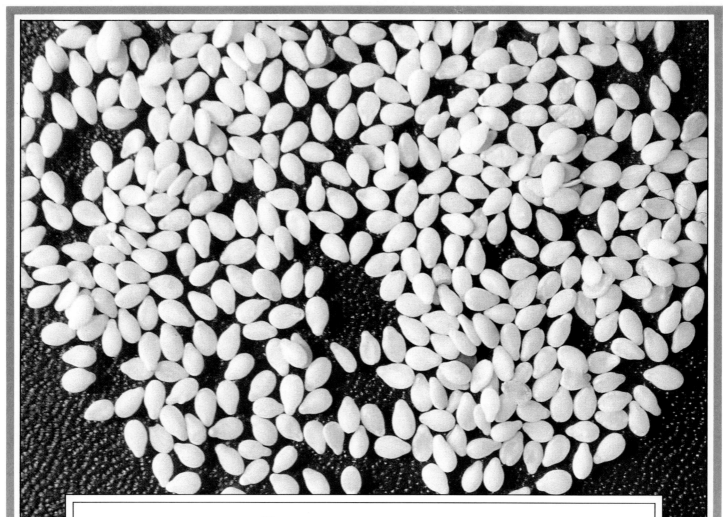

— SESAME SEED —

To WONDER the great cave could only be opened when one of the forty thieves cried 'Open Sesame.' Sesame is one of the most beneficial of seeds to humanity, especially in the Middle East. It originated in that important crossroad between Europe, Asia and Africa and was mentioned in Egyptian writings almost 4,000 years ago. Today sesame seeds are cultivated everywhere in the sub-tropical world but especially in India, China, Mexico and the Middle East. Their primary use is in the production of vegetable oil, but the seeds have many other culinary uses.

Virtually everywhere they are sprinkled on food to add an extra bit of flavour and appeal. In India they are used in curries and other sauces.

Halva, *the* sweetmeat of the Levant is crushed sesame seeds, as is tahina or tahini, which is eaten daily with pita bread.

The Romans, the Greeks, in fact just about everyone in all periods sprinkled the seeds on breads and pastries. They are terrific to have in the kitchen. The only problem seems to be how quickly they run out.

Over the millennia, a sort of sesame seed literature has grown up. Early herbals claimed the seeds to be an antidote to the bite of the spotted lizard. So, if that happens to be your problem, take note. The Roman writer Pliny claimed that the seeds cause bad breath, but, the most bizarre tale of all was told by the Greek historian Herodotus. It seems that a local tyrant had ordered 300 boys to be castrated. On the journey the boys escaped from their guards and found sanctuary in a temple. They outlasted the siege of their angry guards by subsisting on the local peasants religious offerings of sesame seed cakes. Ultimately, the boys managed to return to their homes intact. Now, there must be a lesson in that, mustn't there?

— SESAME SEED —

Chicken Breasts with Sesame Seeds

SERVES 6

INGREDIENTS

2 eggs
fresh rosemary, chopped
black pepper, freshly ground
30 g/2 tbsp fine matzo meal
45 g/3 tbsp sesame seeds
1 kg/2¼ lb chicken breasts (boneless), cut into small pieces
vegetable oil for frying

PREPARATION

♦ Mix the eggs, rosemary and black pepper.
♦ Mix the matzo meal and sesame seeds.
♦ Dip pieces of the chicken into the egg then the sesame mixture.
♦ When the oil is sizzling put in the chicken pieces.
♦ When the chicken is golden brown on one side, sprinkle generously with pepper and turn, sprinkling the other side when it has browned as well.
♦ Drain on kitchen paper (paper towel) and serve.

— SESAME SEED —

Bean Sprouts Korean Style

SERVES 4-6

INGREDIENTS

2¾ cups/200 g/8 oz bean sprouts
10 ml/2 tsp corn, sunflower or sesame oil
2 spring onion (scallion) tails
½ cup/100 ml/4 fl oz water
10 g/2 tsp Sesame Seed Powder (see below)
10 g/2 tbsp salt
1 red pepper (capsicum)

PREPARATION

♦ Wash the bean sprouts and drain them.
♦ Heat the oil in a wok or shallow saucepan.
♦ Chop the spring onion tails into rings.
♦ Cook and stir the bean sprouts and spring onion tails together in the wok or saucepan with the sesame seed powder and salt until the bean sprouts are tender.
♦ Place the cooked vegetables on a serving dish and decorate them with strips of red pepper.

Serve with satay or any oriental style meat or fish dish.

Sesame Crunch

MAKES 10

INGREDIENTS

½ cup/100 g/4 oz butter or margarine
30 ml/2 tbsp golden syrup (corn syrup)
2 tbsp/25 g/1 oz brown sugar
2 cups/150 g/6 oz rolled oats
30 g/2 tbsp sunflower seeds
15 g/1 tbsp coconut flakes or carob drops
oven temperature 190°C/375°F/Gas 5

PREPARATION

♦ Heat the butter and syrup until the butter has melted.
♦ Take off the heat and stir in the rest of the ingredients.
♦ Put the mixture into a greased tin (pan) and press down. Bake in the oven and cook for 30-40 minites or until brown.
♦ Remove the crunch from the oven, leave it to cool for 10 minutes and then cut it into squares in the tin. Wait for it to cool completely before taking the crunch out of the tin.

Hummus

INGREDIENTS

1½ cups/150 g/6 oz chick peas (garbanzos)
4 cloves, garlic crushed
juice of 1 lemon
½ cup/100 g/4 oz tahini paste
15 ml/1 tbsp olive oil

GARNISH

30 ml/2 tbsp olive oil
paprika, a pinch
3 sprigs of parsley, chopped

PREPARATION

♦ Wash the chick peas and soak overnight. Rinse and cook in unsalted water until soft, approximately 1 hour. Retain the cooking liquid.
♦ Liquidize the chick peas with garlic, lemon juice, tahini paste, a tablespoon of olive oil and 4 tbsp of the chick pea water.
♦ If the paste is too thick add a little more water, until it has the consistency of mayonnaise. Add garlic and lemon juice to taste.
♦ Chill the mixture. Serve on a flat dish, smooth the top and garnish with paprika and chopped parsley. Pour over the remaining olive oil. Serve with pitta bread.

Sesame Seed Powder

INGREDIENTS

sesame seeds

PREPARATION

♦ Wash any quantity of seeds carefully and drain them.
♦ Roast them slowly in a dry frying pan, turning constantly until the seeds are a light brown.
♦ Remove the seeds from the heat and pulverize them in a pestle and mortar.
♦ Store the sesame seed powder in airtight conditions out of the light.

—STAR ANISE—

S TAR ANISE is not only the most beautiful spice to behold, but is an architectural marvel of nature. It is not related to aniseed but their essential oils, and thus aromas, are almost identical. These essential oils form the basis of flavouring for a number of liqueurs, chiefly Anisette and Pernod. This spice originated in southern China or northern Vietnam and is cultivated throughout South-east Asia. By far its greatest use is in Chinese cooking. In fact, that characteristic aroma of the Chinese restaurant is mainly star anise.

Chinese chefs would consider it unthinkable to prepare most duck and pork dishes without it.

Most of all, star anise figures in the Chinese five spices mix, a subtle and useful combination that is well worth having on your shelf. It is simply equal parts of five ground spices. They are:
♦ Szechuan pepper *Zanthoxylum piperitum*, which you will have to buy at a Chinese food shop
♦ Cassia (in America, cinnamon really is cassia)
♦ Cloves
♦ Fennel seed
♦ Star anise

Remember, a pinch is all that is needed. If you must substitute for Szechuan pepper, use half the quantity of white peppercorns and half crushed chillis (chilis).

Prawn Stir Fry

SERVES 4

INGREDIENTS

2 tbsp/30 ml cooking oil
2 dried red chillis (chilis), finely chopped
4 cloves garlic, crushed
6 tsp/30 ml/4 fl oz soy sauce
1½ cups/200 g/½ lb frozen peeled prawns (or shrimp)
thawed and drained
½ cup/50 g/2 oz unsalted cashew nuts
2 cups/100 g/4 oz mushrooms, sliced
5 stalks celery, diced
10 cm/4 in cucumber, peeled and diced
⅓ Chinese cabbage, diced
¼ Cos (Romaine) lettuce, diced
2.5 cm/1 in piece fresh ginger, finely chopped
a pinch of five spice powder (see page 110)
6 spring onions (shallots), finely chopped
6 cups/400 g/1 lb bean sprouts

PREPARATION

◆ Heat 1 tbsp/15 ml of the oil in a wok. Add the chillis, 1 clove of garlic and ½ tsp/2½ ml soy sauce.
◆ Add the prawns and stir fry. Add the cashews and stir fry for a few seconds. Remove the prawns and cashews and set aside.
◆ Stir fry the mushroom, celery, cucumber, cabbage and lettuce, plus 4½ tsp/22½ ml soy sauce. Remove and set aside.
◆ Put the rest of the oil in the wok, then add the remaining garlic, the ginger and the five spice powder.
◆ Add the bean sprouts and 1 further tsp/5 ml of soy sauce. Stir fry. Add all the other ingredients and mix well. Serve immediately.

— STAR ANISE —

Peking Duck

SERVES 4

INGREDIENTS
FIRST MARINADE
1 1.5 kg/3 lb duck
6 spring onions (scallions)
90 ml/6 tbsp wine
30 ml/2 tbsp soy sauce
SECOND MARINADE
4 slices fresh ginger
16 cloves
4 cloves star anise
2 fennel roots

PREPARATION

♦ Wash and dry the duck.
♦ Crush the spring onions and add the remaining ingredients of the first marinade.
♦ Place the spring onions only inside the duck, rub the marinade all over the outside of the duck and leave it for 2 hours.
♦ Remove the spring onions and put in their place 2 slices of ginger.
♦ Spread the spring onions, the other 2 slices of ginger and the other ingredients of the second marinade on and around the duck.
♦ Steam the duck for an hour, cool it and drain it.
♦ Heat almost enough oil to cover the duck in a deep frying pan.
♦ Once the oil is hot, remove the pan from the heat and place the duck gently in it, taking care not to burn yourself. Spoon the oil over the duck and fry until the duck is browned all over, returning it to the heat only if the oil cools down too much.

Serve with pickles and sauce.

The Pickle

INGREDIENTS
1 cucumber
5 g/1 tsp salt
10 g/2 tsp sugar
1 chilli (chili), cut into strips
1 onion, sliced
15 ml/1 tbsp vinegar

PREPARATION

♦ Slice the cucumber lengthways, remove its seeds and cut it into strips. Add the salt and set aside for 15 minutes. Rinse well and dry.
♦ Add the sugar, chilli and onion slices. Pour on the vinegar last.

The Sauce

INGREDIENTS
15 g/1 tbsp salted soybeans, crushed
5 ml/1 tsp soy sauce
5 ml/1 tsp sesame oil
5 g/1 tsp sugar
5 ml/1 tsp water

PREPARATION

♦ Combine all the ingredients together and steam over a low heat for 10 minutes.

— STAR ANISE —

Chicken Soup South East Asian Style

SERVES 8

INGREDIENTS
SOUP
400 g/1 lb beef
1 medium size chicken
5 g/1 tsp lengkuas
2 star anise
10 cloves
$\frac{1}{2}$ grated nutmeg
8 peppercorns
5 g/1 tsp salt
5 g/1 tsp sugar (optional)
10 shallots, sliced and fried
10 cloves garlic, sliced and fried
GARNISHES
20 shallots, sliced and fried
1 bunch spring onions (scallions)
1 cup/100 g/$\frac{1}{4}$ lb Chinese celery, sliced
$1\frac{1}{2}$ cups/100 g/4 oz bean sprouts
CUTLETS
1 cup/200 g/8 oz minced (ground) beef
4 cups/400 g/16 oz potatoes, boiled and mashed
2 eggs
5 g/1 tsp salt
pepper to taste
sprinkling of nutmeg
vegetable oil for frying

PREPARATION

♦ Boil 4$\frac{1}{2}$ cups/1 l/1$\frac{3}{4}$ pts water, add the beef and simmer until tender. Remove the beef and slice it finely.
♦ Add a further 9 cups/2 l/3$\frac{1}{2}$ pts water to the beef stock and bring it to the boil.
♦ Add the chicken and cook it over a medium heat. Remove the chicken when cooked, approximately an hour, and rinse it in cold water.
♦ Shred the meat off the bones and place to one side, return the bones to the stock.
♦ Add the spices and two thirds of the cooked shallots and garlic.
♦ Simmer for 20 minutes and strain.
♦ To make the cutlets, mix all the ingredients and the remaining shallots and garlic from the soup.
♦ Shape them into patties and fry until they are golden brown.
♦ Place the bean sprouts, chicken, beef slices and cutlets into individual bowls and pour the hot soup over them.

Serve with Chinese celery and spring onions.

— TURMERIC —

TURMERIC is a root or rhizome which is related to ginger. When the root is halved the very deep yellow interior is revealed. Undoubtedly, this sun coloured root fascinated the ancients because from the earliest times it was associated with magic. In Hindu ceremony, it represents fertility. Turmeric originated in India, but now is cultivated throughout South-east Asia and Jamaica. On account of its musty aroma and yellow colour, the spice is an essential ingredient in curry powders. It is employed widely in any number of culinary applications where the yellow colour is important, pickles and piccalilli, for example.

Turmeric is an important spice on its own; however, in no circumstances should it be substituted for saffron. Not only do the two spices differ widely in flavour and aroma, but in chemical attributes. Saffron, for example, is extremely soluble in water, while turmeric is not. Attempting to make great saffron specialities like *paella* or *Bouillabaisse* with turmeric can only spell disaster.

Turmeric is difficult to grind and will always be sold in its powdered form. It quickly loses its aromatic qualities, so do not buy too much at once.

Two major importers of the spice are Iran and Japan. Iran's festive dishes are often yellow, but it makes one wonder because saffron is a native produce. In the case of Japan, the large importation of turmeric may simply reflect that country's current passion for curry.

— TURMERIC —

Fish in Turmeric

SERVES 4-6

INGREDIENTS

*1 large red mullet, enough for 4-6 (Grey mullet, monk fish or any
other firm fleshed, non-oily fish can be used and may be cheaper)
flesh of one fresh coconut
2 fresh green chillis (chilis)
2.5 cm/1 in piece fresh ginger
$2\frac{1}{2}$ g/$\frac{1}{2}$ tsp white pepper
2 tsp/10 ml turmeric
salt to taste
1 large lemon
oven temperature 180°/350°F/Gas 4*

PREPARATION

◆ Clean and scale fish, but leave whole.
◆ Grate or liquidize all the other ingredients, except the
lemon.
◆ Rub the liquidized paste inside and outside the fish.
◆ Wrap in foil and bake for 25-35 minutes.
◆ Sprinkle with lemon juice and serve with lemon wedges.

— TURMERIC —

Piccalilli

INGREDIENTS

2 kg/4 lb marrow
12 small onions
approx. 5 cups/600 g/1 lb 8 oz French (green) or runner beans
2 doz gherkins, ½ cup/50 g/2 oz
10 g/2 tsp rock salt
4½ cups/1 l/1¾ pt vinegar
30 g/2 tbsp sugar
6 peppercorns
2 medium size pieces of root ginger
5 g/1 tsp Curry Powder (see page 124)
15 g/1 tbsp plain (all-purpose) flour
45 g/3 tbsp turmeric

PREPARATION

♦ Cut the marrow into 2.5 cm (1 in) cubes.
♦ Peel and slice the onions.
♦ Break the cauliflower up into small florets (flowerets).
♦ Cut the beans into 2.5 cm (1 in) lengths.
♦ Wash all the vegetables and spread them out on a large china dish. Sprinkle them with rock salt and leave them for 24 hours.
♦ Rinse and drain the vegetables thoroughly.
♦ Place the vegetables in a large saucepan with nearly all the vinegar and the sugar, and the peppercorns and ginger tied in a muslin (cheesecloth) bag. Simmer gently.
♦ Mix the curry powder, flour and turmeric into a paste with the rest of the vinegar.
♦ Bring the vegetables to the boil and stir in the turmeric paste until smooth. Leave to simmer for 10 minutes.
♦ Remove the ginger.
♦ Bottle and tie down in sterilized jars when cold.

Roast Turkey

SERVES 6-8

INGREDIENTS

4 kg/9 lb turkey
1 green pepper (capsicum), finely chopped
10 g/2 tsp ginger
2 onions, finely chopped
2 cups/350 g/12 oz half-cooked brown rice
30 ml/2 tbsp vinegar
10 g/2 tsp turmeric
10 g/2 tsp black pepper
10 g/2 tsp Garam Masala (see page 124)
oven temperature 170°C/325°F/Gas 3

PREPARATION

♦ Wash the turkey and remove its skin.
♦ For the stuffing, mix together the green pepper, ginger, onions and rice, ½ tsp vinegar and pack it into the bird.
♦ Prepare a paste of turmeric, black pepper, garam masala, and the rest of the vinegar. Rub it onto the bird.
♦ Cover with foil and bake in the oven for 20 minutes for each 400 g.
♦ Baste frequently with butter and the turkey's own fat.
♦ Remove the foil to brown the turkey 20 minutes before taking it out of the oven.

— VANILLA —

*I*T IS IMPOSSIBLE to emphasize the culinary richness handed to us by the pre-Columbian Mexicans. What would ice cream be without their gifts of both chocolate and vanilla. Today, our problem is that real vanilla is hardly ever found in commercial preparations. The food industry insists upon using the artificial vanilla which technologists claim is identical chemcially to the real thing. Once it was not so bad when it was extracted from the eugenol in either clove, cinnamon leaf or pimento oils. Later is was processed from coal-tar extracts, but today most vanillia is produced from paper mill wastes! In any event, as a spice vanillia is distinctly inferior to vanilla itself.

Although the spice now is cultivated throughout the tropical world, the best quality vanilla still comes from Mexico. Do buy and use those wonderful long, brown fresh pods (beans). The very best pods have tiny white crystals, or a 'frost', coating their outsides. Here the flavour is most concentrated.

An ideal place to keep your vanilla pods is stuck right into a jar of sugar. Not only will it keep the vanilla fresh, but the sugar will acquire a bit of extra deliciousness. In our kitchen we need two tall jars of sugar because one is occupied by cinnamon sticks and the other by vanilla.

Although both vanilla and cinnamon traditionally complement chocolate, we have not worked up the courage to try them in the same sugar jar.

— VANILLA —

Vanilla Cream

INGREDIENTS

3 eggs
$\frac{1}{4}$ cup/50 g/2 oz vanilla sugar
1 cup/225 ml/8 fl oz milk
$2\frac{1}{2}$ tsp/$12\frac{1}{2}$ g/$\frac{1}{2}$ oz gelatine (gelatin)
$\frac{1}{4}$ cup/50 ml/2 fl oz water
2 tsp/10 ml vanilla essence (extract) (see page 121)
1 cup/225 ml/8 fl oz double (table) cream

PREPARATION

♦ Beat the eggs and sugar until pale and frothy.
♦ Heat the milk to almost boiling point and pour over the egg mixture.
♦ Strain the mixture back into the saucepan. Simmer over a very low heat or in a double boiler until thick, stirring all the time.
♦ Allow to cool.
♦ Soak the gelatine in water for 5 minutes, then heat to dissolve.
♦ Stir the vanilla essence into the cooled custard, followed by the gelatine.
♦ Whip the cream and fold into the mixture before it sets.
♦ Pour into a dish and refrigerate.

— Vanilla —

Iced Coffee

INGREDIENTS

2½ cups/500 ml/1 pt strong strained coffee
1⅐ cups/250 ml/½ pt cold milk
¼ cup/30 g/2 oz sugar (optional)
2.5 ml/½ tsp vanilla essence (extract)
50-75 ml/2-3 tbsp double (heavy) cream

PREPARATION

♦ Mix all the ingredients together. Drink when well chilled.

Vanilla Slices

INGREDIENTS

150 g/6 oz puff pastry
⅔ cup/150 ml/¼ pt double (heavy) cream
5 ml/1 tsp vanilla essence (extract)
1¼ cups/175 g/6 oz raspberries
white glacé icing flavoured with vanilla
oven temperature 230°C/450°F/Gas 8

PREPARATION

♦ Roll the puff pastry until it is an even ½ cm (¼ in) thick. Cut into strips 10 cm (4 in) in width.
♦ Bake for 20 minutes. Allow to cool.
♦ Whip the cream adding the vanilla essence.
♦ Clean and wash the raspberries.
♦ Using 2 or 3 slices of baked pastry, make sandwiches with the whipped cream and raspberries as the filling.
♦ Top each slice with a little vanilla glacé icing. Delicious!

Oatmeal Cookies

MAKES 36

INGREDIENTS

½ cup/100 g/4 oz margarine
½ cup/100 g/4 oz brown sugar
salt (optional)
1 egg, slightly beaten
7.5 ml/1½ tsp vanilla essence (extract)
2 cups/200 g/8 oz fine wholewheat flour
3.5 g/¾ tsp baking powder
2⅓ cups/400 g/16 oz wheat germ
7 cups/600 g/1 lb 8 oz rolled oats
1 cup/175 g/6 oz sunflower seeds or chopped nuts
1 cup/175 g/6 oz raisins (optional)
oven temperature 190°C/350°F/Gas 5

PREPARATION

♦ Cream together the margarine, sugar and salt.
♦ Mix in the egg and the vanilla.
♦ Sift the flour and baking powder.
♦ Mix the flour with the wheat germ and rolled oats.
♦ Blend together the dry and liquid ingredients.
♦ Add a spoonful of water if the mixture is too thick.
♦ Place tablespoon-size portions of the batter onto a well-greased pan.
♦ Bake for 10-12 minutes, or until golden brown.

— SAUCES —

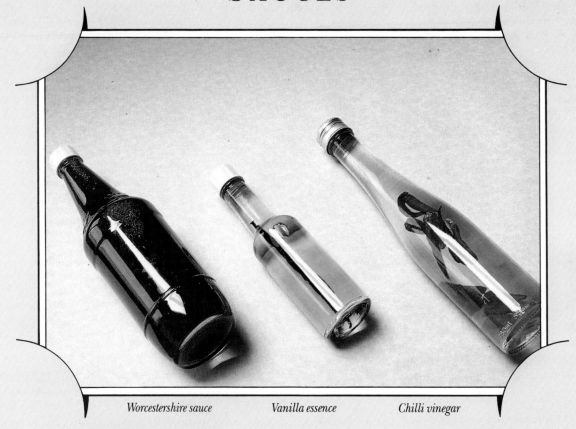

Worcestershire sauce   Vanilla essence   Chilli vinegar

Worcestershire Sauce

INGREDIENTS
6 cloves garlic, crushed
5 g/1 tsp black pepper
$1\frac{1}{4}$ g/$\frac{1}{4}$ tsp chilli (chili) powder
$\frac{1}{3}$ cup/75 ml/3 oz soy sauce
$1\frac{1}{2}$ cups/350 ml/12 fl oz vinegar

PREPARATION

♦ Liquidize ingredients. Store in an airtight bottle. Shake well before use.

Garlic Paste

INGREDIENTS
2 bulbs garlic
a few drops of olive oil
ghee (clarified butter)

PREPARATION

♦ Crush the garlic thoroughly with the oil.
♦ When the paste forms a smooth, thick mass, pack into a small jar. Cover with ghee and foil.

Horseradish Sauce

INGREDIENTS
15 g/1 tbsp freshly grated horseradish
$\frac{1}{4}$ pt double (table) cream
few drops of olive oil

PREPARATION

♦ Mix horseradish and cream together.
♦ Add the olive oil.

Chilli (Chili) Vinegar

INGREDIENTS
$1\frac{1}{2}$ tbsp red hot chilli (chili)
$2\frac{1}{2}$ cups/$\frac{1}{2}$ l/1 pt vinegar

PREPARATION

♦ Steep the chilli in the vinegar. Shake daily for 10 days.
♦ Strain and bottle.

—SAUCES—

Bechamel sauce Garlic paste Horseradish sauce Mustard mayonnaise

Bechamel Sauce

MAKES ½ LITRE

INGREDIENTS
4 tbsp/2 oz butter or margarine
2 tbsp/12 g/½ oz flour
2 cup/375 ml/¾ pt milk
salt and pepper to taste
nutmeg, if required

PREPARATION

♦ Melt butter or margarine in saucepan.
♦ Stir in the flour.
♦ Take off the heat and add a little of the milk. Return to a low heat, add the rest of the milk, a little at time. Never stop stirring.
♦ Still stirring, cook for another 10 minutes, adding salt and pepper.

Vanilla Essence (Extract)

INGREDIENTS
2 vanilla pods
1 cup/225 ml/10 oz brandy

PREPARATION

♦ Partially break vanilla pods and put into the brandy. Leave in an airtight bottle for 6 weeks, shaking every day.

Mustard Mayonnaise

INGREDIENTS
½ tbsp/7½ ml Dijon mustard
1 egg yolk
½ tsp/2½ ml Worcestershire Sauce (see page 120)
1 tsp/5 ml white wine vinegar
salt and freshly ground pepper
several drops of tabasco sauce
1 cup/225 ml/8 fl oz sunflower oil
juice of half a lemon

PREPARATION

♦ Blend together the Dijon mustard, egg yolk, Worcestershire sauce, vinegar, salt and pepper, tabasco sauce and a small amount of oil.
♦ Add the rest of the oil slowly, still blending.
♦ Add the lemon juice.

— DRINKS —

Vodka in Aniseed   *Tequila Maria*

Vodka in Aniseed

INGREDIENTS
30 g/2 tbsp coriander seeds
15 g/1 tbsp fennel seeds
45 g/3 tbsp anise seeds
½ cup/100 g/4 oz sugar
2½ cups/500 ml/20 fl oz vodka

PREPARATION

♦ Grind or crush seeds.
♦ Add the seeds and sugar to the vodka.
♦ Shake vigorously every day for a week.
♦ Strain and bottle.

Saké Maria

INGREDIENTS
½ cup/100 ml/4 fl oz juice
juice of 1 lemon
tabasco sauce to taste
freshly ground pepper
¼ cup/50 ml/2 fl oz saké

PREPARATION

♦ Mix all ingredients with crushed ice in a large tumbler.
Serve with a stalk of celery.

Tequila Maria

INGREDIENTS
a generous pinch of white pepper
a generous pinch of celery salt
tabasco sauce to taste
a dash of Worcestershire Sauce (see page 120)
a pinch of oregano
juice of a fresh lime/lemon
2½ g/½ tsp freshly grated horseradish
¼ cup/50 ml/2 fl oz Tequila
½ cup/100 ml/4 fl oz tomato juice

PREPARATION

♦ Stir all ingredients briskly in a large tumbler with crushed
ice.

— DRINKS —

Mulled Wine

INGREDIENTS

1 orange sliced
1 lemon, sliced
1 cinnamon stick
10 cloves
$1\frac{1}{4}$ g/$\frac{1}{4}$ tsp ginger
$\frac{1}{4}$ nutmeg, grated
3 tbsp/45 ml/$1\frac{1}{2}$ oz dark brown sugar
2 cups/500 ml/1 pt red wine
$\frac{1}{2}$ cup/100 ml/4 fl oz brandy
$1\frac{1}{4}$ cups/250 ml/$\frac{1}{2}$ pt water

PREPARATION

♦ Put the fruit, spices and sugar into the bottom of a pan.
♦ Add the wine, brandy and water.
♦ Gradually heat to just boiling point.
♦ Adjust flavouring to taste.
♦ Simmer gently until ready to use.

Do *not* boil as that will destroy the alcoholic content.

Spiced Punch

INGREDIENTS

1 bottle claret
peel of 1 orange
6 cloves
1 cinnamon stick
3 cardamom pods, crushed
3 coriander seeds, crushed
15 g/1 tbsp bruised root ginger

PREPARATION

♦ Put all ingredients in a bowl and leave for 8 hours.
♦ Strain and heat until wine starts to ripple.
♦ Do not allow to boil.

— Spice Mixes —

Garam masala 1 Curry Powder 1 Garam masala 2 Curry Powder 2 Old fashioned garam masala

HEN INDIVIDUAL spices are combined the aromatic result of the mixture is often greater than the sum of the parts. Heat all seeds in the oven or in a frying pan until a rich aroma is given off. Coriander and cumin seeds should not be heated in the same pan. Use an electric grinder. A coffee grinder will work well. Because of lingering aromas some people have a grinder specifically for the task. Sieve well. Store in an airtight jar, in dry, dark and cool conditions.

These mixes actually improve day by day for the first few weeks after grinding, but then they start losing potency, so, do not make too much at once.

The numbers beside the spices indicate proportions.

Curry Powder Mixes

MIX ONE
Cumin   1
Coriander   4
Fenugreek $\frac{1}{2}$
Turmeric $1\frac{1}{2}$
Black pepper $\frac{1}{2}$
Cardamom $\frac{1}{4}$
Chilli (chili)   1
(can vary to desired heat)

MIX TWO
Black pepper   1
Cloves   1
Cinnamon   2
Cardamom   1
Coriander   6
Cumin   2
Fenugreek $\frac{1}{2}$
Nutmeg   1
Chilli (chili)   2

Garam Masala

MIX ONE
Cinnamon   2
Black pepper   3
Cloves   2
Cumin   2
Mace   1
Cardamom seeds   1
Bay leaves   2

MIX TWO
Black cumin seeds   3
Coriander $7\frac{1}{2}$
Cardamom   4
Bay leaves $\frac{1}{2}$
Cloves   5
Black pepper   5
Nutmeg $1\frac{1}{2}$
Mace $1\frac{1}{2}$
Cinnamon   4

— SPICE MIXES —

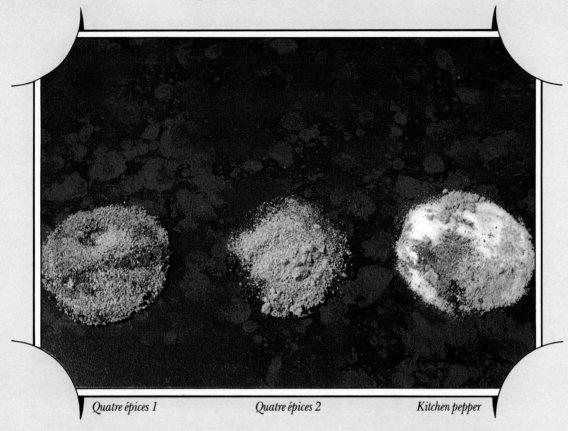

Quatre épices 1   Quatre épices 2   Kitchen pepper

Quatre Epices

This famous French spice blend is popular in charcuterie products, however, it can be used as a general seasoning when extra bite is needed. White pepper is the main ingredient.

MIX ONE

White pepper   7
Allspice   3
Mace   1
Nutmeg $\frac{1}{2}$
Cloves $\frac{1}{3}$
Cinnamon $\frac{1}{2}$

(We know there are six spices. Nutmeg and mace are essentially the same spice and the allspice just makes it a bit better!)

MIX TWO

White pepper   7
Nutmeg   1
Cloves   1
Ginger   1

Kitchen Pepper

This mixture is wonderful in sauces.

Salt   10
Ginger   4
White pepper   1
Mace   1
Cloves   1
Nutmeg   1

Old Fashioned Philadelphia Spice Powder

Try seasoning a pork roast with this $2\frac{1}{2}$ hours before cooking, or just sprinkle some on steaks, sauces, stuffings or baked ham.

MIXTURE

Cloves   2
Nutmeg   1
Mace   1
Cayenne pepper   1
Basil   1
Thyme   1
Bay leaf   1

— INDEX —

A

Africa, 7, 8-9, 57, 72, 90, 93, 107
aioli, 66
Allium sativum, 64
allspice, 6, 10, 12, 14-16, 93, 97
  Curried goat, 15
  honey cake, 15
  Pickled red cabbage, 15
  spice cake, 16
  spiced vinegar, 15
  see also pimento
Amsterdam, 77
anethole, 17
aniseed, 17, 110
  Anise cookies, 18
  Carrot and sweet potato
    tzimmes, 19
  Spiced Indian tea, 19
  Vodka in aniseed, 122
apple: Apple cake, 40
  Apple tart with cinnamon sticks, 39
  Horseradish and apple sauce, 76
Arabs, 7, 8, 9, 23, 43, 49, 103
Arawaks, 97
Artichokes (Jerusalem) with savoury
  rice, 31
Asia, 8, 107
Asia Minor, 100
Assam, 8
Atlantic Ocean, 9, 10-11
aubergine: Babagannouch, 52-3
  Parsee dhansak, 58
  Ratatouille, 47
Australia, 72
Austria, 87
Aztecs, 34

B

Babagannouch, 52-3
Baked ham, 43
banana: Banana cake, 28
  Banana custard, 86
  Chicken curry, 56
Banda, 9, 10
Bangladesh, 8
bean curd (tofu): Curried bean curd
  burgers, 56
bean sprouts: Bean sprouts Korean
  style, 109
  Chicken soup south east Asian
    style, 113
  Prawn stir fry, 111
Beaumont, Francis, 72
Bechamel sauce, 121
beef: Chicken soup south east Asian
  style, 113
  Koftas, 61
  Meat loaf, 89
  Meat patties, 78
  Parsee dhansak, 58
  Seekh kebab, 47
  Spiced brisket, 93, 99
  Steak and stout, 94
  Steak au poivre verte, 93
beer: Steak and stout, 94
beetroot: Horseradish with
  beetroot, 76
Bible, 7, 8, 52, 64
Big sur soup, 67
biscuits: Oatmeal cookies, 119
  Easter biscuit, 105
  Sesame crunch, 109
black peppercorns, *see* pepper, black
Borneo, 9

bouillabaisse, 103, 114
brandy: mulled wine, 123
  Vanilla essence, 121
Brazil, 90, 95
Bread sauce, 79
bream: Fish cutlets, 89
brisket, spiced, 93, 99
Brown fish stew, 99
Bulgaria, 45
bulgur wheat: Chilli ordinaire, 33
burgers, curried bean curd, 56
Burgundy, 82
buttermilk: Kalan, 56

C

cakes: Apple cake, 40
  Banana cake, 28
  Dream bars, 27
  Hamantaschen, 100, 102
  Honey cake, 15
  Lemon and clove cake, 43
  Orange ginger bread, 71
  Parkin brownies, 27
  Poppy seed crunch, 102
  Seed cake, 21
  Spice cake, 16
  Vanilla slices, 119
calamus, 7
California, 64
Cambridgeshire, 103
Canada, 82
cannelloni, 85
Cappucino coffee, 38
capsicum, 10, 29, 87
  see also chilli
Capsicum anum, 29
Capsicum fruitescens, 29
caraway, 20-2
  Potato soup, 21
  Satay sauce, 22
  Seed cake, 21
cardamom, 6, 23-5
  Cardamom coffee, 24
  Coconut cream toffee, 24
  Firnee, 25
  Honey milk, 24
  Spiced omelette, 24
Caribbean, 43, 97
cassia, 6, 7, 8, 26-8, 110
  Banana cake, 28
  Dream bars, 27
  Parkin brownies, 27
  Plantain tarts, 27
cayenne, 29-31, 87
  Artichokes with savoury rice, 31
  Devilled turkey legs, 31
  Tomato juice, 31
  Tuna paté, 30
Central America, 10
Chaucer, Geoffrey, 8-9
cheese: Cannelloni, 85
  Cheese soufflé, 96
  Garlic onion soup, 67
  Gnocchi, 42
  Omelette with cheese and
    horseradish, 75
  Risotto, 105
  Veal clou de girofle, 43
  Welsh rarebit, 81
chick peas: Felafel, 51
  Hummus, 109
  Spinach and chick pea salad, 95
chicken: Chicken breasts with
  sesame seeds, 108
  Chicken curry, 56

Chicken garam masala, 62
Chicken soup south east Asian
  style, 113
  Koftas, 61
  Paella, 103, 104
  Simple mole, 35
Chicory and walnut salad, 58
Chile, 10
chilli, 6, 10, 29, 32-7, 87
  Chilli con carne, 32, 87
  Chilli crab, 33
  Chilli ordinaire, 33
  Chilli vinegar, 120
  Crisped shrimps, 36
  Cucumber raita, 63
  Goa prawn curry, 59
  Mole poblano, 34
  Onion salad, 34
  Simple mole, 35
  Yucatan soup, 37
China, 8, 26, 41, 45, 69, 80, 107, 110
Chinese celery: Chicken soup
  south east Asian style, 113
Chinese lettuce, *see* coriander
chocolate, 38, 117
  Simple mole, 34, 35
Chopped liver, 98
Cinnamomum zeylanicum, 26
cinnamon, 6, 7-8, 12, 26, 38-40, 90,
  110, 117
  Apple cake, 40
  Apple tart with cinnamon sticks, 39
  Date jam, 40
  Sweet potato pie, 40
clams: Paella, 103, 104
cloves, 6, 8-9, 10-11, 12, 41-4, 90, 110
  Baked ham, 43
  Bread sauce, 79
  Gnocchi, 42
  Khitichree, 44
  Lemon and clove cake, 43
  Veal clou de girofle, 43
coconut: Coconut cream toffee, 24
  Crisped shrimps, 36
  Dream bars, 27
  Fish in turmeric, 115
  Kalan, 56
  Satay sauce, 22
coffee, 38
  Cardamom coffee, 24
  Iced coffee, 119
Colman, J. & J., 12, 82
Columbus, Christopher, 9-10
cookies, *see* biscuits
coriander, 45-8, 124
  Fresh coriander new potatoes, 46
  Masoor dal, 47
  Ratatouille, 47
  Seekh kebab, 47
  Spicy bean salad, 48
Cornwall, 105
Cortez, 34
courgette: Kalan, 56
  Ratatouille, 47
crab: Chilli crab, 33
  Devilled crabmeat, 82
cream: Ginger and rhubarb fool, 70
  Vanilla cream, 118
  Vanilla slices, 119
  Veal clou de girofle, 43
cream, sour: Veal goulash, 88
Crisped shrimps, 36
cucumber: cucumber raita, 63
  Peking duck, 112
  Smoked mackerel and cucumber
    sauce, 79
  Spicy bean salad, 48

cumin, 20, 49-53, 124
  Babagannouch, 52-3
  Felafel, 51
  Lentil soup, 52
  Tahini cream salad, 51
  Tandoori sole, 50
Curnonsky, 84
currants: Easter biscuit, 105
curry, 54-6, 114
  Chicken curry, 56
  Curried bean curd burgers, 56
  Curried goat, 15
  Curry powder, 60, 124
  Goa prawn curry, 59
  Kalan, 56
  Pork curry, 55
  see also garam masala
custard, banana, 86

D

Date jam, 40
desserts: Banana custard, 86
  Ginger and rhubarb fool, 70
  Vanilla cream, 118
Devilled crabmeat, 82
Devilled turkey legs, 31
Dijon, 12, 82
dips: Hummus, 109
  Tahini cream salad, 51
Dream bars, 27
drinks: Mulled wine, 123
  Orange punch, 86
  Orange tropical, 86
  Pineappleade, 71
  Saké Maria, 122
  Spiced punch, 123
  Tequila Maria, 122
  Tomato juice, 31
  Vodka in aniseed, 122
duck: Peking duck, 112
  roast, 89

E

East Africa, 8, 57
Easter biscuit, 105
eggplant, *see* aubergine
eggs: Omelette with cheese and
  horseradish, 75
  Spiced omelette, 24
Egypt, 7, 17, 64, 66, 100, 107
England, 11, 12, 80, 82, 103, 105
Escoveitched fish, 92
eugenol, 41, 117
Exodus, 7

F

Felafel, 51
fennel, 17, 110
fenugreek, 57-9
  Chicory and walnut salad, 58
  Fenugreek potatoes, 58
  Goa prawn curry, 59
  Parsee dhansak, 58
Firnee, 25
fish: Brown fish stew, 99
  Escoveitched fish, 92
  Fish cutlets, 89
  Fish in turmeric, 115
  Salmon loaf, 92

Smoked mackerel and cucumber sauce, 79
Tandoori sole, 50
Tuna paté, 30
Yucatan soup, 37
Five spices mix, 110
Florida, 93
fool, ginger and rhubarb, 70
France, 11, 12, 26, 41, 43, 64, 66, 74, 77, 80, 82, 93, 95, 103
French bean salad in mustard sauce, 82
Fresh coriander new potatoes, 46

G

Gama, Vasco da, 9
garam masala, 23, 60-3, 124
  Chicken garam masala, 62
  Cucumber raita, 63
  Koftas, 61
  Samosas, 61
garbanzos, see chick peas
garlic, 6, 7, 64-8
  aioli, 66
  Garlic onion soup, 67
  garlic paste, 120
  Moules in garlic, 65
  Potatoes à la garlic, 68
  Scallops, 66
  Worcestershire sauce, 120
Germany, 74, 80, 82, 93, 103, 105
ginger, 6, 8, 10, 36, 69-73, 90, 114
  Ginger and rhubarb fool, 70
  Ginger syrup sauce, 71
  Melon cocktail, 71
  Orange ginger bread, 71
  pineappleade, 71
Gnocchi, 42
Goa prawn curry, 59
goat, curried, 15
goulash, 87
  veal, 88
Granada, 43
Greece, 49, 57, 69, 100, 107
green peppercorns, see pepper, green
grey mullet: Fish in turmeric, 115
Guatemala, 23
Gyorgi, Szent, 87

H

halva, 107
ham, baked, 43
Haman, 100
Hamantaschen, 100, 102
Henry VIII, 12
Henry, Prince of Portugal, 9
Herodotus, 7, 107
Hindus, 54, 114
Holland, 11, 41, 43, 77
honey: Baked ham, 43
  Honey cake, 15
  Honey milk, 24
horseradish, 10, 74-6
  Horseradish and apple sauce, 76
  Horseradish sauce, 120
  Horseradish with beetroot, 76
  Mayonnaise with horseradish, 76
  Omelette with cheese and horseradish, 75
  Potato salad with horseradish, 76
Hummus, 109
Hungary, 87

I

Iced coffee, 119
India, 7, 8, 9, 10, 23, 29, 41, 49, 52, 54, 57, 60, 72, 87, 90, 100, 105, 107, 114
Indian Ocean, 8, 9
Indonesia, 9, 26, 43, 90
Iran, 103, 105, 114
Islam, 54, 66
Israel, 64

J

jackfish: Brown fish stew, 99
jam, date, 40
Jamaica, 9, 14, 54, 72, 97, 114
Japan, 36, 54, 80, 114
Jerusalem artichokes, see artichokes
Jews, 74, 100, 102

K

Kalan, 56
Kampuchea, 90
Kashmir, 103
kebabs: seekh kebab, 47
Khasi Hills, 8
Khitichree, 44
kichlach, onion, 92
kid: Curried goat, 15
Kitchen pepper, 125
Koftas, 61

L

lamb: curried, 15
  Koftas, 61
  Meat loaf, 89
lemon: Babagannouch, 52-3
  Lemon and clove cake, 43
lentils: Khitichree, 44
  Lentil soup, 52
  Masoor dal, 47
  Parsee dhansak, 58
Levant, 107
liver, chopped, 98
long pepper, 90

M

mace, 6, 12, 77-9, 90
  Bread sauce, 79
  Mashed turnips, 79
  Meat patties, 78
  Smoked mackerel and cucumber sauce, 79
mackerel: Smoked mackerel and cucumber sauce, 79
Madagascar, 43
Magellan, Ferdinand, 10-11
Malabar, 90
Malagasy Republic, 43
Malaysia, 8, 90
La Mancha, 103
Marseilles, 103
Mashed turnips, 79
Masoor dal, 47
Massachusetts, 12
mayonnaise: aioli, 66
  Mayonnaise with horseradish, 76
  Mustard mayonnaise, 121
  see also sauces

Meat loaf, 89
Meat patties, 78
Mediterranean, 7, 9, 17, 49, 93, 103
Melon cocktail, 71
Mexico, 10, 34, 36, 38, 107, 117
Middle East, 23, 52, 57, 105, 107
mignonette pepper, 95
milk: Firnee, 25
  Honey milk, 24
  Iced coffee, 119
Mole poblano, 34
Moluccas, 9, 10-11, 41, 43
monk fish: Fish in turmeric, 115
Montezuma, 34
Morocco, 45
Moses, 64
Moslems, 54, 66
Moules in garlic, 65
Mulled wine, 123
mushrooms: Steak and stout, 94
mussels: Moules in garlic, 65
  Paella, 103, 104
mustard, 10, 12, 36, 74, 80-3
  Devilled crabmeat, 82
  Devilled turkey legs, 31
  French bean salad in mustard sauce, 82
  Mustard mayonnaise, 121
  Russian salad, 83
  Welsh rarebit, 81
myristicin, 84
myrrh, 7

N

New England, 12
New Guinea, 9
Nigeria, 72
Nile valley, 52
noodles, poppy seed, 101
nutmeg, 6, 8-9, 10-11, 12, 77, 84-6, 90
  Banana custard, 86
  Cannelloni, 85
  Orange punch, 86
  Orange tropical, 86
nuts: Hamantaschen, 100, 102
  Oatmeal cookies, 119

O

oatmeal: Oatmeal cookies, 119
  Parkin brownies, 27
  Sesame crunch, 109
Old fashioned Philadelphia spice powder, 125
omelettes: Omelette with cheese and horseradish, 75
  Spiced omelette, 24
onion: Escoveitched fish, 92
  Garlic onion soup, 67
  Onion kichlach, 92
  Onion salad, 34
orange: Orange ginger bread, 71
  Orange punch, 86
  Orange tropical, 86

P

paella, 103, 104, 114
paprika, 87-9
  Fish cutlets, 89
  Meat loaf, 89
  Roast duck, 89

Veal goulash, 88
Parkin brownies, 27
Parsee dhansak, 58
Passover, 74
pastries: Vanilla slices, 119
paté, tuna, 30
patties, meat, 78
peanuts: Satay sauce, 22
peas: Samosas, 61
Peking duck, 112
Pennsylvania, 105
pepper, black, 6, 7, 9-10, 12, 36, 90-2
  Escoveitched fish, 92
  Onion kichlach, 92
  Salmon loaf, 92
  Tomato salad, 91
pepper, green, 93-4
  Spiced brisket, 93
  Steak and stout, 94
  Steak au poivre verte, 93
pepper, red, 93
  Spiced brisket, 93
pepper, white, 95-6
  Cheese soufflé, 96
  Spinach and chick pea salad, 95
peppers, 10
  Escoveitched fish, 92
  Ratatouille, 47
  Veal goulash, 88
Persia, 100
Philadelphia spice powder, 125
Philistines, 64
Phoenicians, 105
Piccalilli, 116
pickles: for Peking duck, 112
  Piccalilli, 116
  Pickled red cabbage, 15
pimento, 6, 97-9
  Brown fish stew, 99
  Chopped liver, 98
  Spiced brisket of beef, 99
  see also allspice
Pineappleade, 71
Piper longum, 90
Piper nigrum, 90, 93
Plantain tarts, 27
Pliny the Younger, 7-8, 107
Poivre, Pierre, 43
Poland, 14
poppy seed, 100-2
  Hamantaschen, 100, 102
  Poppy seed crunch, 102
  Poppy seed noodles, 101
pork: Koftas, 61
  Meat loaf, 89
  Pork curry, 55
Portugal, 9, 10, 11, 41
potato: Chicken soup south east Asian style, 113
  Fenugreek potatoes, 58
  Fresh coriander new potatoes, 46
  Potato salad with horseradish, 76
  Potato soup, 21
  Potatoes à la garlic, 68
  Samosas, 61
potato, sweet, see sweet potato
prawns: Goa prawn curry, 59
  Prawn stir fry, 111
Provence, 66
punch, Spiced, 123

Q

Quatre epices, 125

—INDEX—

R

raisins: Oatmeal cookies, *119*
raita, cucumber, *63*
raspberry: Vanilla slices, *119*
Ratatouille, *47*
Red cabbage, pickled, *15*
red kidney beans: Spicy bean salad, *48*
red mullet: Brown fish stew, *99*
  Escoveitched fish, *92*
  Fish in turmeric, *115*
red peppercorns, *see* pepper, red
Red Sea, *7*
relishes: Cucumber raita, *63*
rhubarb and ginger fool, *70*
rice: Artichokes with savoury rice, *31*
  Firnee, *25*
  Khitichree, *44*
  Paella, *103, 104*
  Risotto, *105*
  Saffron rice, *106*
  Stuffing for roast turkey, *116*
ricotta cheese: Cannelloni, *85*
Risotto, *105*
Roast duck, *89*
Roast turkey, *116*
Romania, *45*
Romans, *7-8, 9, 17, 41, 52, 57, 69, 80, 90, 100, 107*
Russian salad, *83*

S

safflower, *105*
saffron, *12, 103-6, 114*
  Easter biscuit, *105*
  Paella, *103, 104*
  Risotto, *105*
  Saffron rice, *106*
Saffron Walden, *103*
Saké Maria, *122*
salads: Chicory and walnut salad, *58*
  French bean salad in mustard sauce, *82*
  Onion, *34*
  Potato salad with horseradish, *76*
  Russian salad, *83*
  Spicy bean salad, *48*
  Spinach and chick pea salad, *95*
  Tahini cream salad, *51*
  Tomato salad, *91*
Salem, *12*
Salmon loaf, *92*
Samosas, *61*
Satay sauce, *22*
sauces: Bechamel, *121,*
  Bread, *79*
  Chilli vinegar, *120*
  Cucumber, *79*
  Garlic paste, *120*
  Ginger syrup sauce, *71*
  Horseradish, *120*
  Horseradish and apple, *76*
  Mustard, *82*
  for Peking duck, *112*
  Satay, *22*
  Worcestershire, *120*
  see also mayonnaise
scallops, *66*
Scandinavia, *14, 23, 38, 66*
Schinus terebinthifolius, 93
Schwenkfelder cake, *105*
scurvy, *87*
Seed cake, *21*
Seekh kebab, *47*

semolina: Gnocchi, *42*
sesame seed, *107-9*
  Bean sprouts Korean style, *109*
  Chicken breasts with sesame seeds, *108*
  Hummus, *109*
  Sesame crunch, *109*
  Sesame seed powder, *109*
Shakespeare, William, *77*
shrimps, crisped, *36*
Sierra Leone, *72*
Silk Route, *8*
Simple mole, *35*
Singapore, *20*
Smoked mackerel and cucumber sauce, *79*
snapper: Brown fish stew, *99*
  Escoveitched fish, *92*
sole, Tandoori, *50*
soufflé, cheese, *96*
soups: Big sur soup, *67*
  Chicken soup south east Asian style, *113*
  Garlic onion soup, *67*
  Lentil, *52*
  Potato, *21*
  Yucatan soup, *37*
South America, *10, 11, 29, 93*
South-east Asia, *69, 110, 114*
Soviet Union, *14, 45*
soy sauce, Peking duck, *112*
  Worcestershire sauce, *120*
soybeans: Peking duck, *112*
Spain, *9, 10-11, 12, 29, 34, 66, 97, 103, 105*
Spice cake, *16*
Spice Islands, *9, 41*
spice mixes, *124-5*
  Curry powder, *124*
  Garam masala, *124*
  Kitchen pepper, *125*
  Old fashioned Philadelphia spice powder, *125*
  Quatre epices, *125*
Spiced brisket, *93, 99*
Spiced punch, *123*
Spiced vinegar, *15*
Spicy bean salad, *48*
spinach: Cannelloni, *85*
  Parsee dhansak, *58*
  Spinach and chick pea salad, *95*
squid: Paella, *103, 104*
Sri Lanka, *23, 26, 29, 38, 90*
star anise, *17, 110-13*
  Chicken soup south east Asian style, *113*
  Peking duck, *112*
  Prawn stir fry, *111*
Steak and stout, *94*
Steak au poivre verte, *93*
sunflower seeds: Oatmeal cookies, *119*
Sweet potato pie, *40*
sweets: Coconut cream toffee, *24*
syrup: Ginger syrup sauce, *71*
Szechuan pepper, *110*

T

tahini, *107*
  Hummus, *109*
  Tahini cream salad, *51*
Taiwan, *72*
Tandoori chicken, *49*
Tandoori sole, *50*

Tanzania, *43*
tarts: Apple tart with cinnamon sticks, *39*
  Plantain tarts, *27*
Tequila Maria, *122*
Texas, *32*
Thailand, *72*
Tibet, *66*
toast: Welsh rarebit, *81*
toffee, coconut cream, *24*
tofu, *see* bean curd
tomato: Paella, *103, 104*
  Ratatouille, *47*
  Simple mole, *35*
  Tequila Maria, *122*
  Tomato juice, *31*
  Tomato salad, *91*
  Yucatan soup, *37*
Tuna paté, *30*
Turkey, *49, 87, 103*
turkey: Devilled turkey legs, *31*
  Roast turkey, *116*
turmeric, *6, 105, 114-16*
  Fish in turmeric, *115*
  Piccalilli, *116*
  Roast turkey, *116*
turnips, mashed, *79*

U

Uganda, *36*
United States of America, *12, 26, 32, 64, 80, 105*

V

vanilla, *6, 117-19*
  Iced coffee, *119*
  Oatmeal cookies, *119*
  Vanilla cream, *118*
  Vanilla essence, *121*
  Vanilla slices, *119*
veal: Veal clou de girofle, *43*
  Veal goulash, *88*
vegetables: Chilli ordinaire, *33*
  Piccalilli, *116*
  Prawn stir fry, *111*
Venice, *9*
Vietnam, *26, 90, 110*
vinegar: Chilli vinegar, *120*
  spiced, *15*
  Worcestershire sauce, *120*
vitamin C, *87*
Vodka in aniseed, *122*

W

walnuts: Chicory and walnut salad, *58*
  Dream bars, *27*
Welsh rarebit, *81*
wheat germ: Oatmeal cookies, *119*
wine: Cucumber sauce, *79*
  Garlic onion soup, *67*
  Moules in garlic, *65*
  Mulled wine, *123*
  Paella, *103, 104*
  Risotto, *105*
  Spiced punch, *123*
Worcestershire sauce, *120*

Y

yoghurt: Cucumber raita, *63*
  Spinach and chick pea salad, *95*
  Tandoori sole, *50*
Yucatan, *36*
Yucatan soup, *37*

Z

Zanthoxylum piperitum, 110
Zanzibar, *43*
zucchini, *see* courgette